PATTERN COLORING BOOK FOR ADULTS

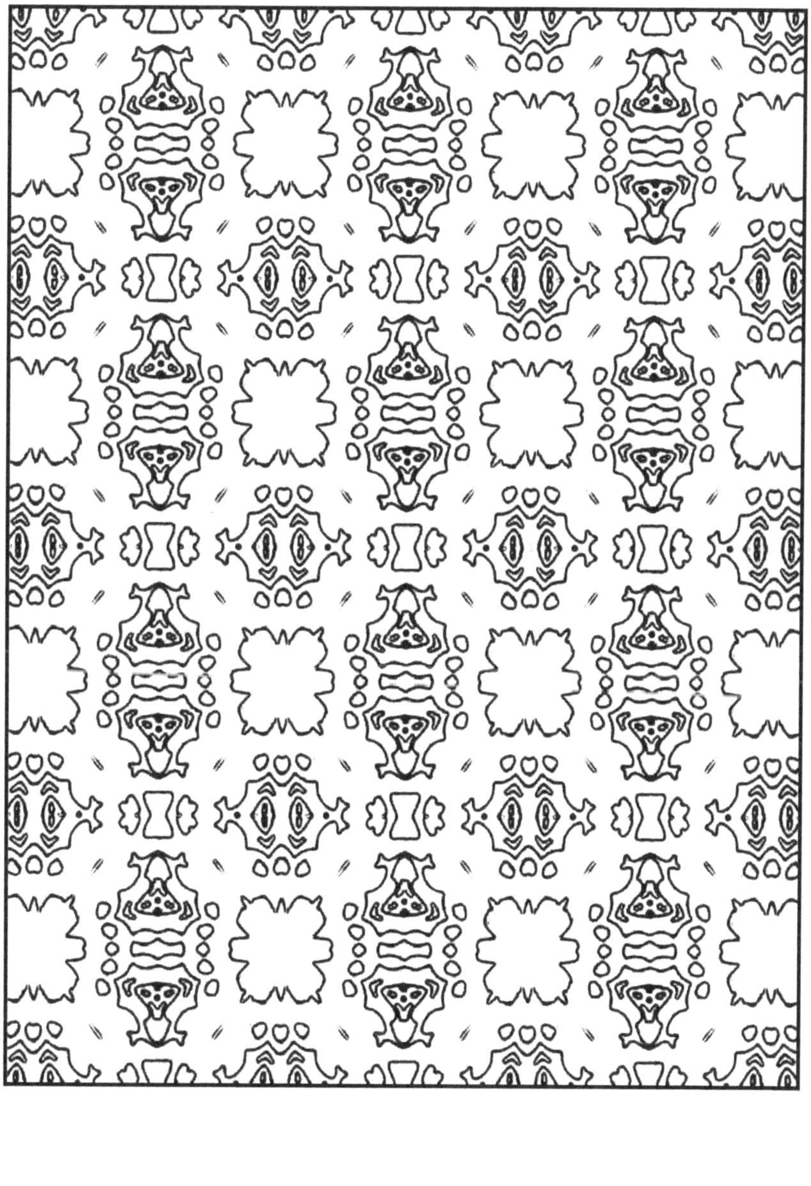

Hours of fun and calming relaxation to color away the stresses of the day

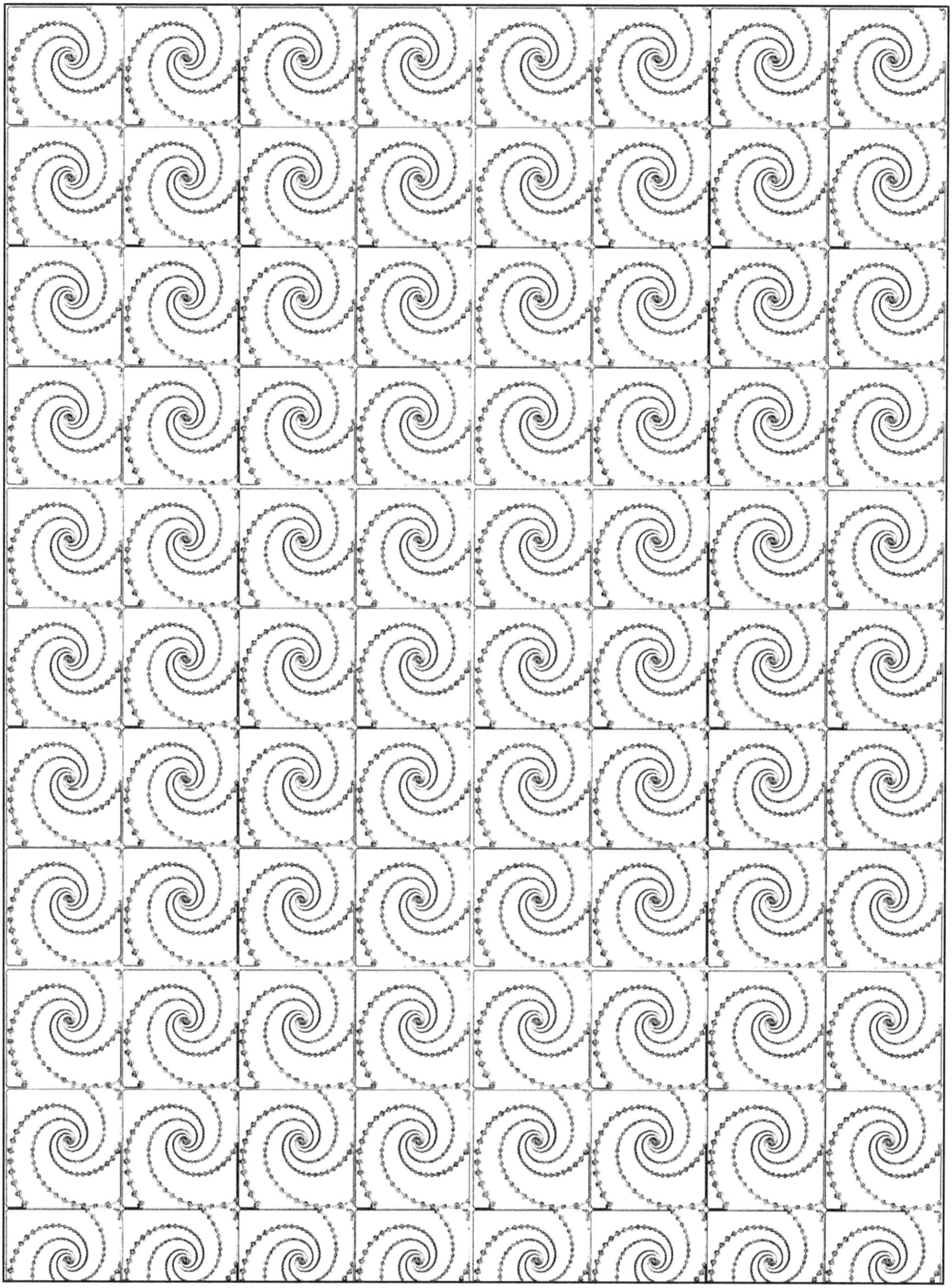

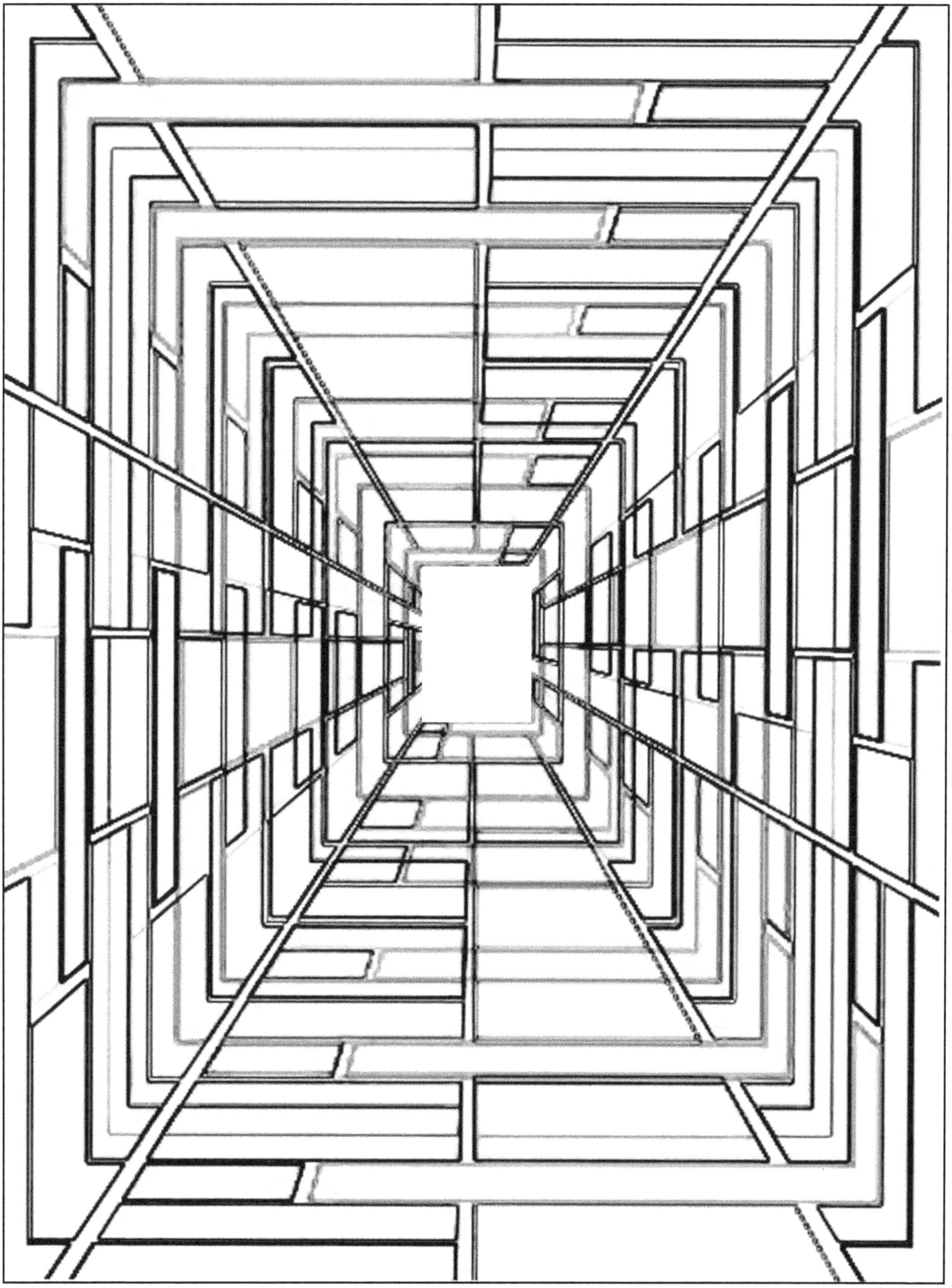

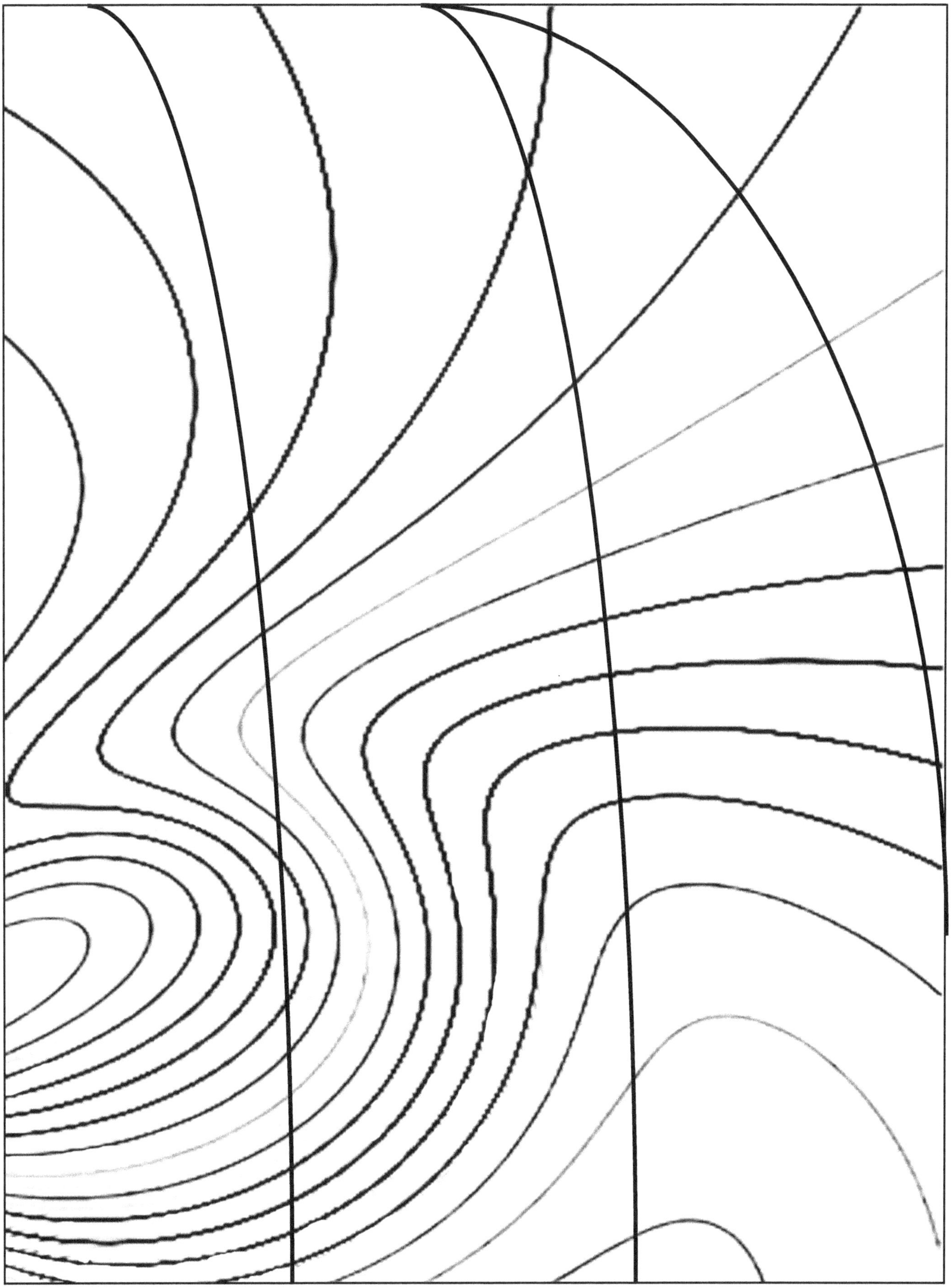

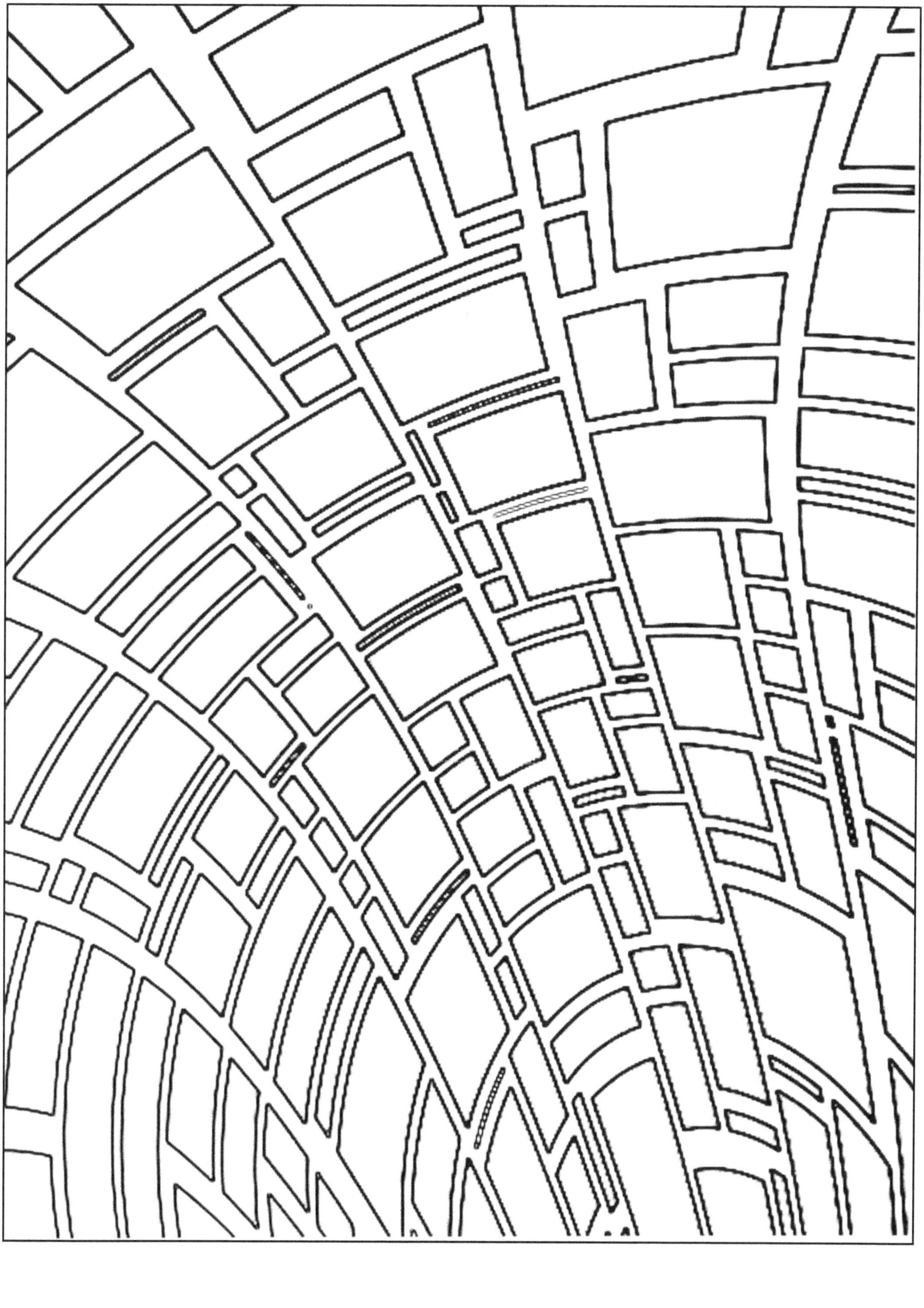

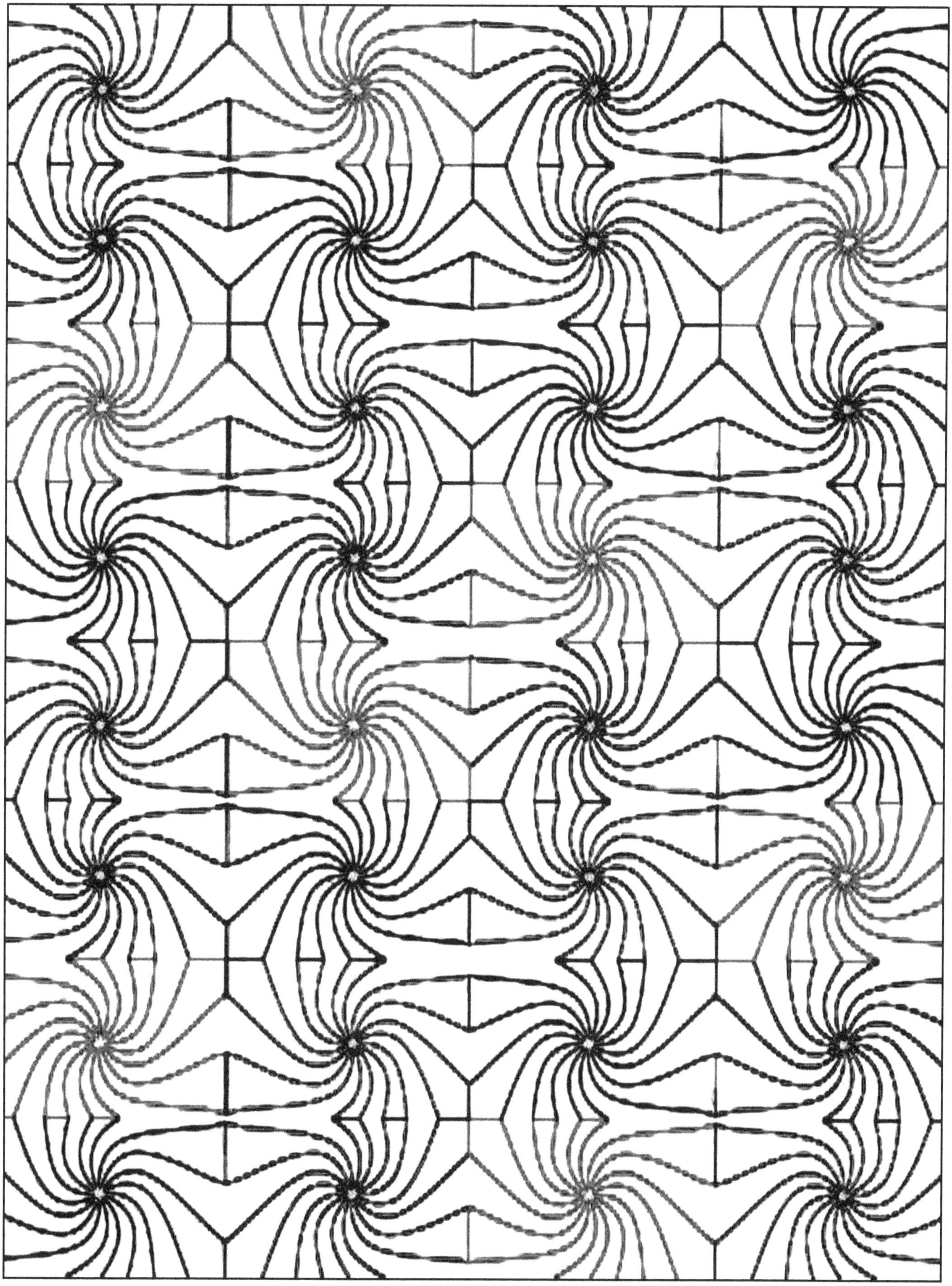

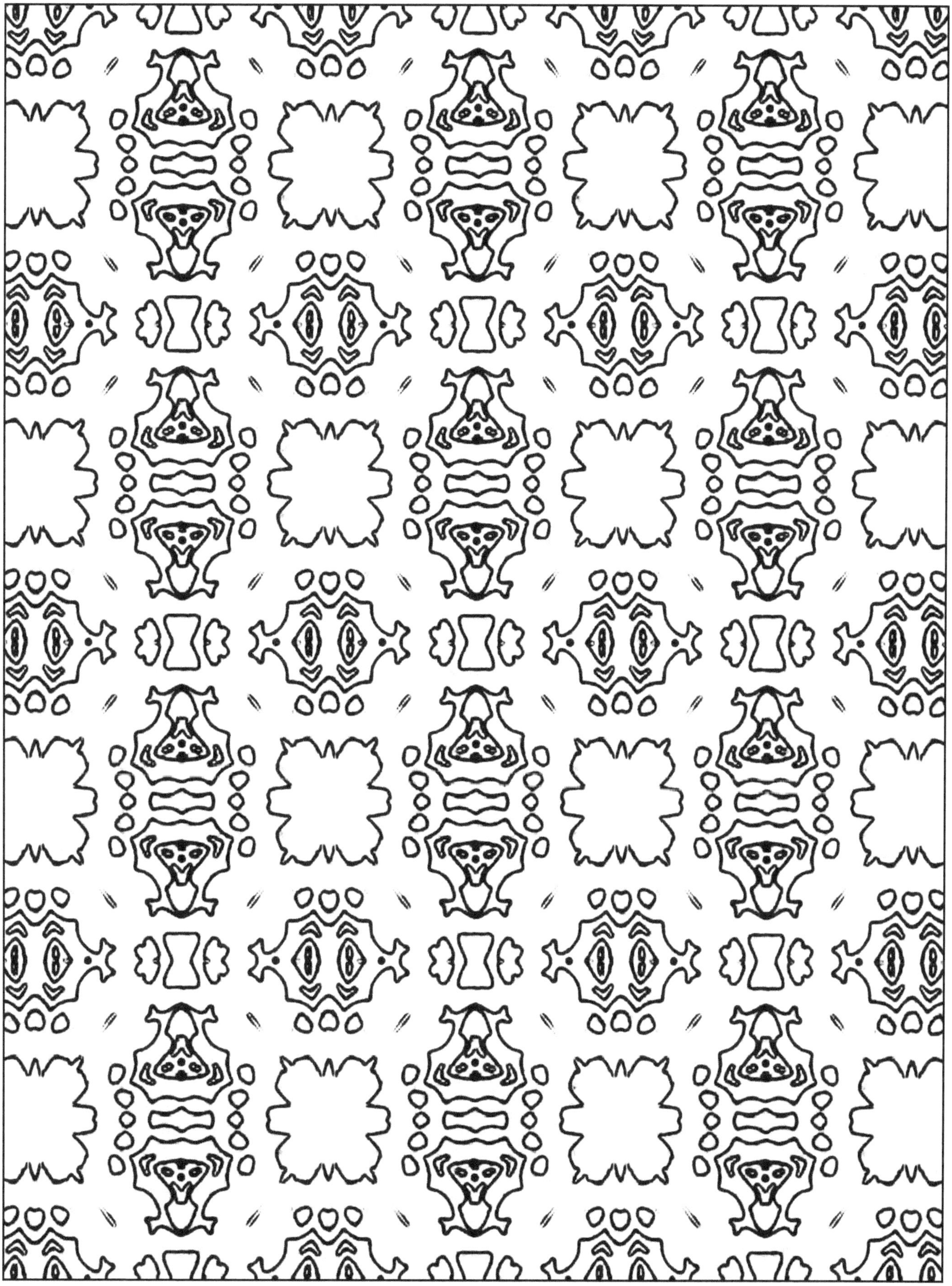

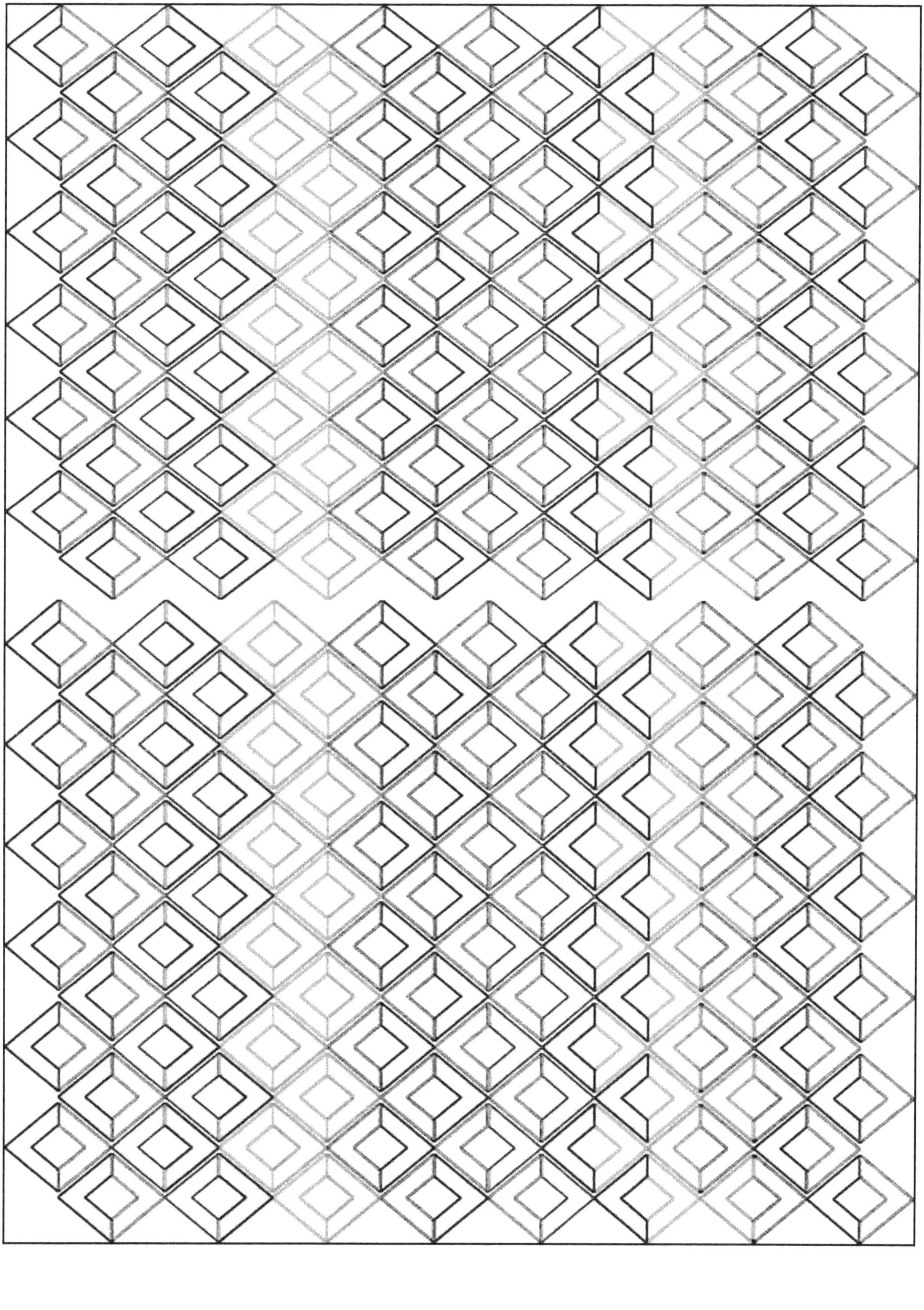

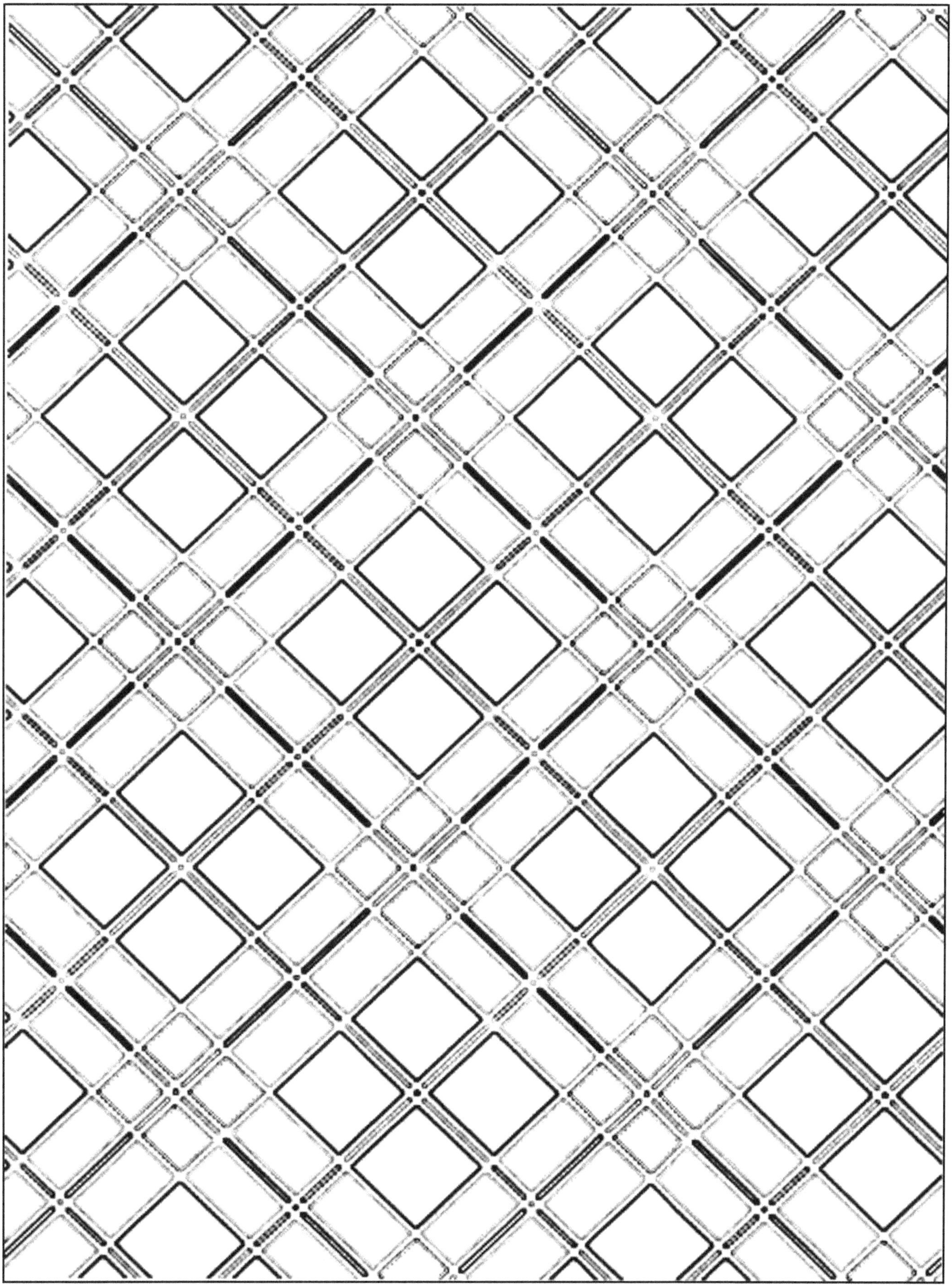

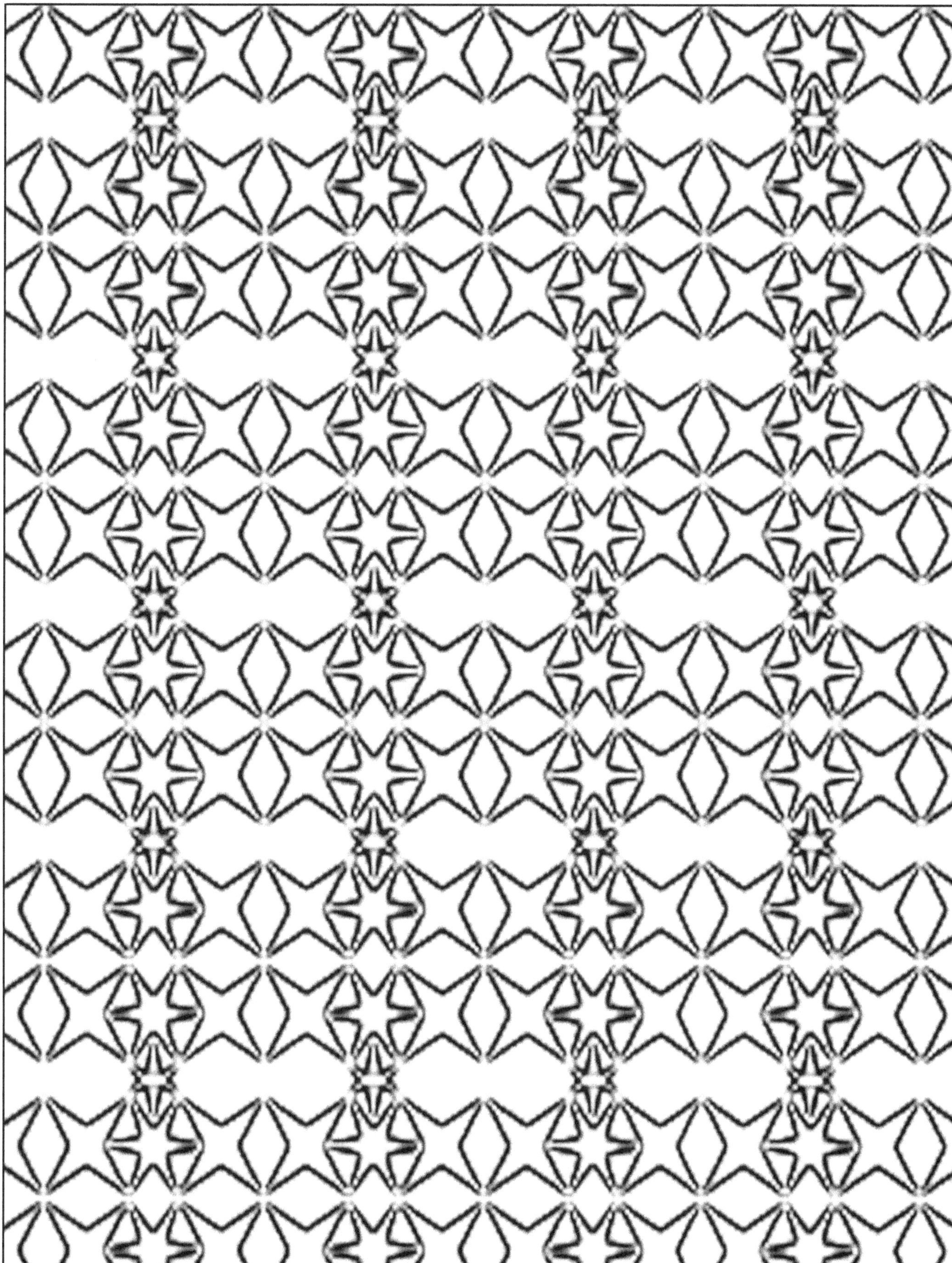

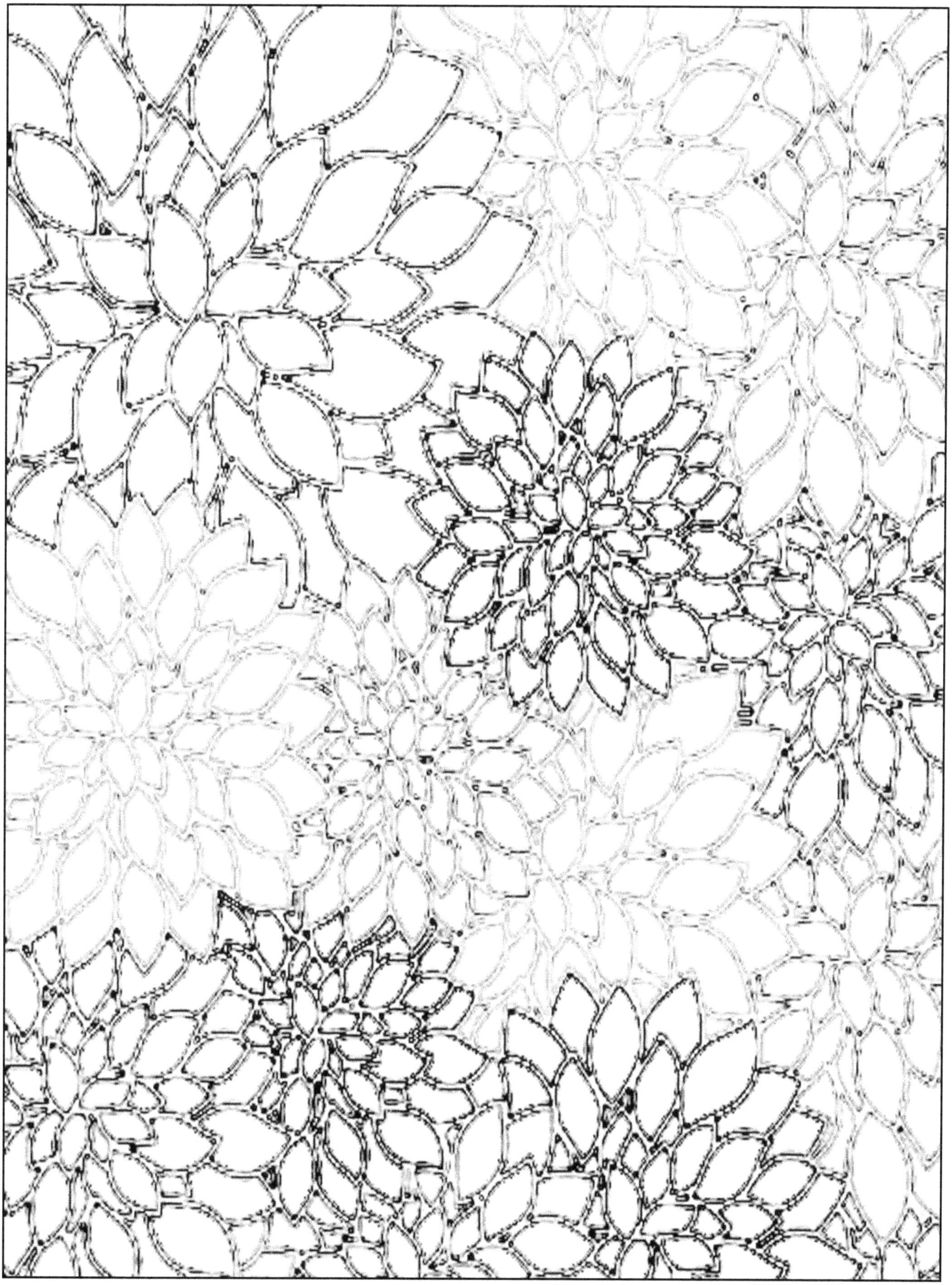

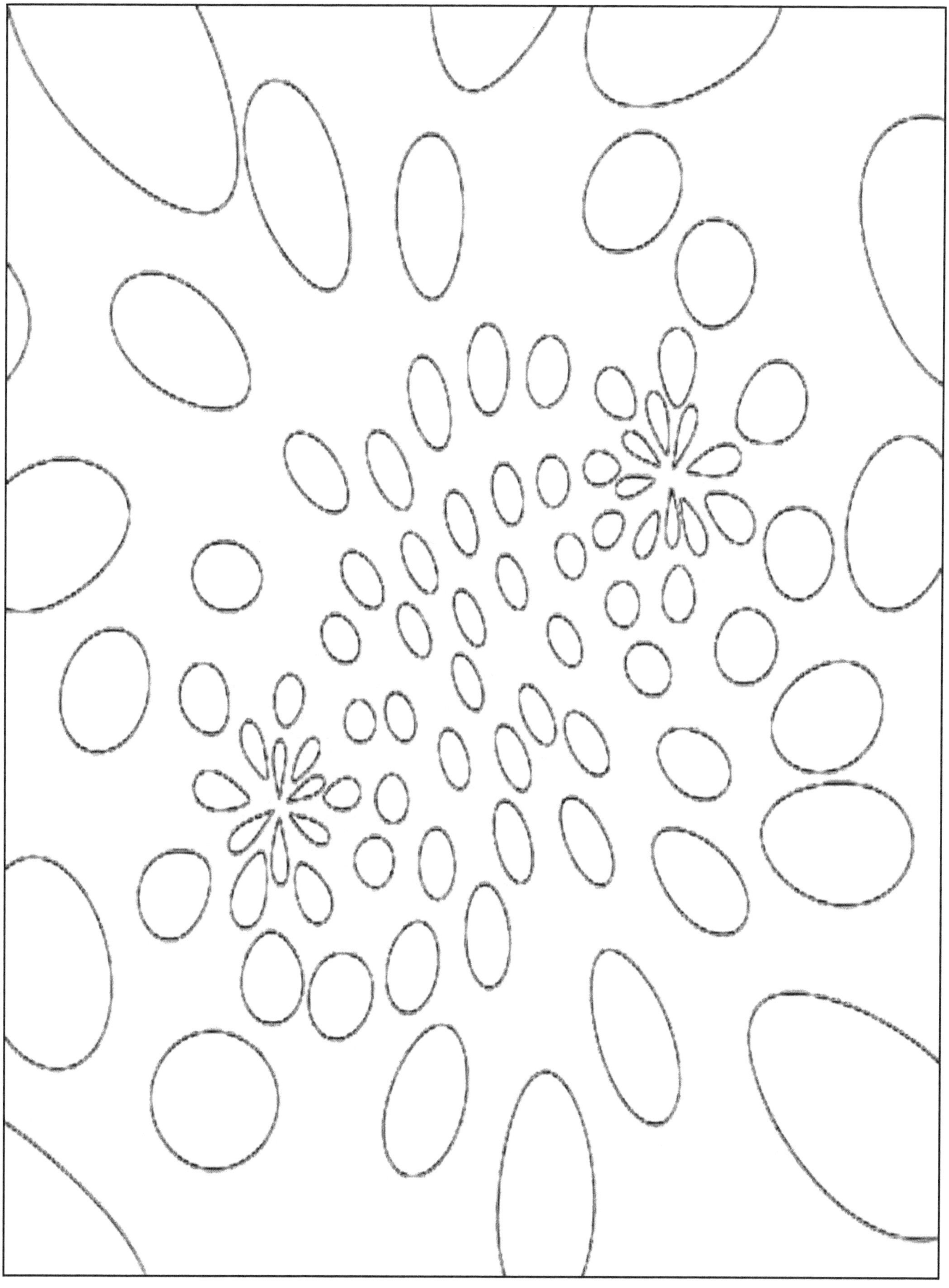

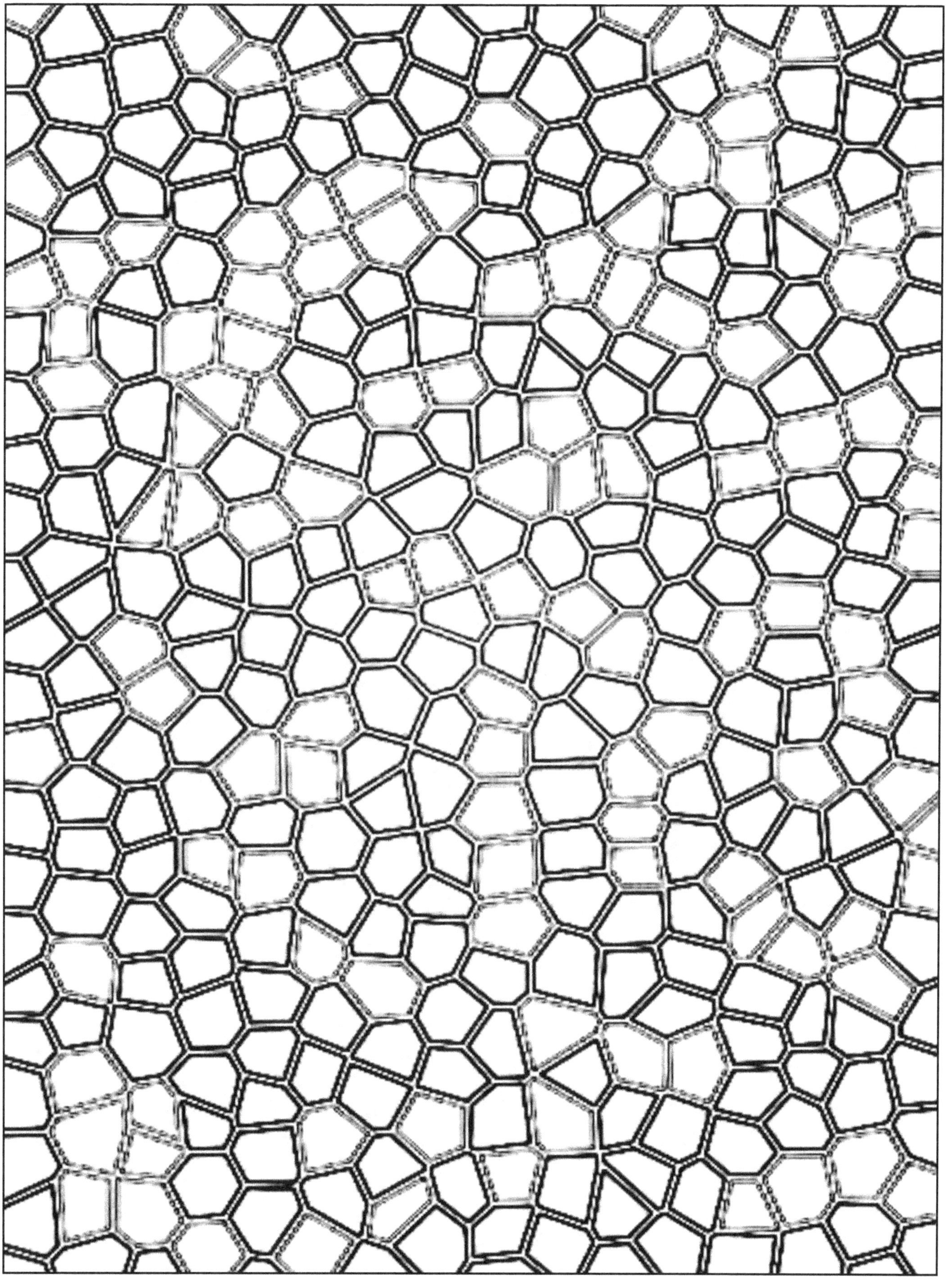

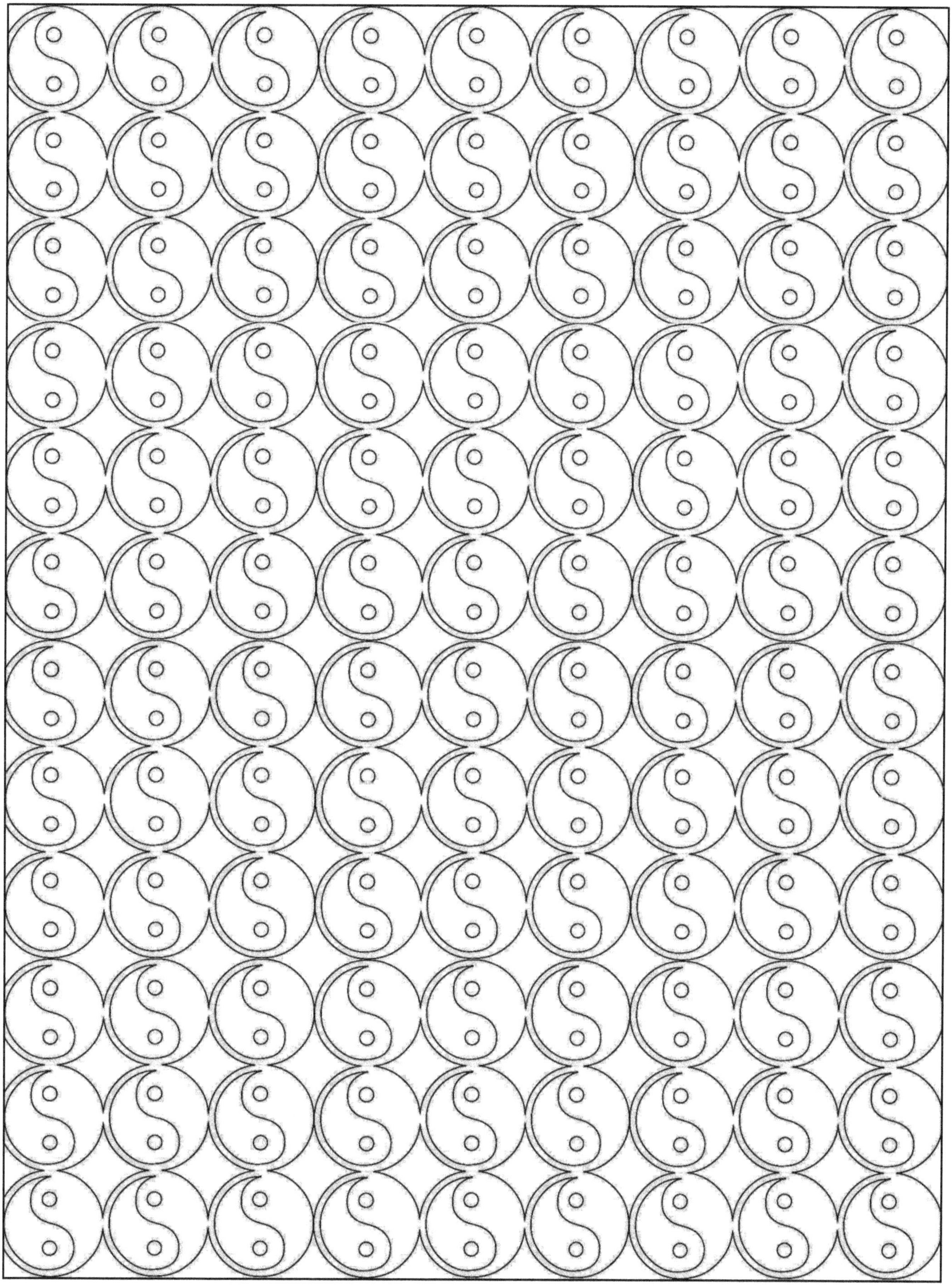

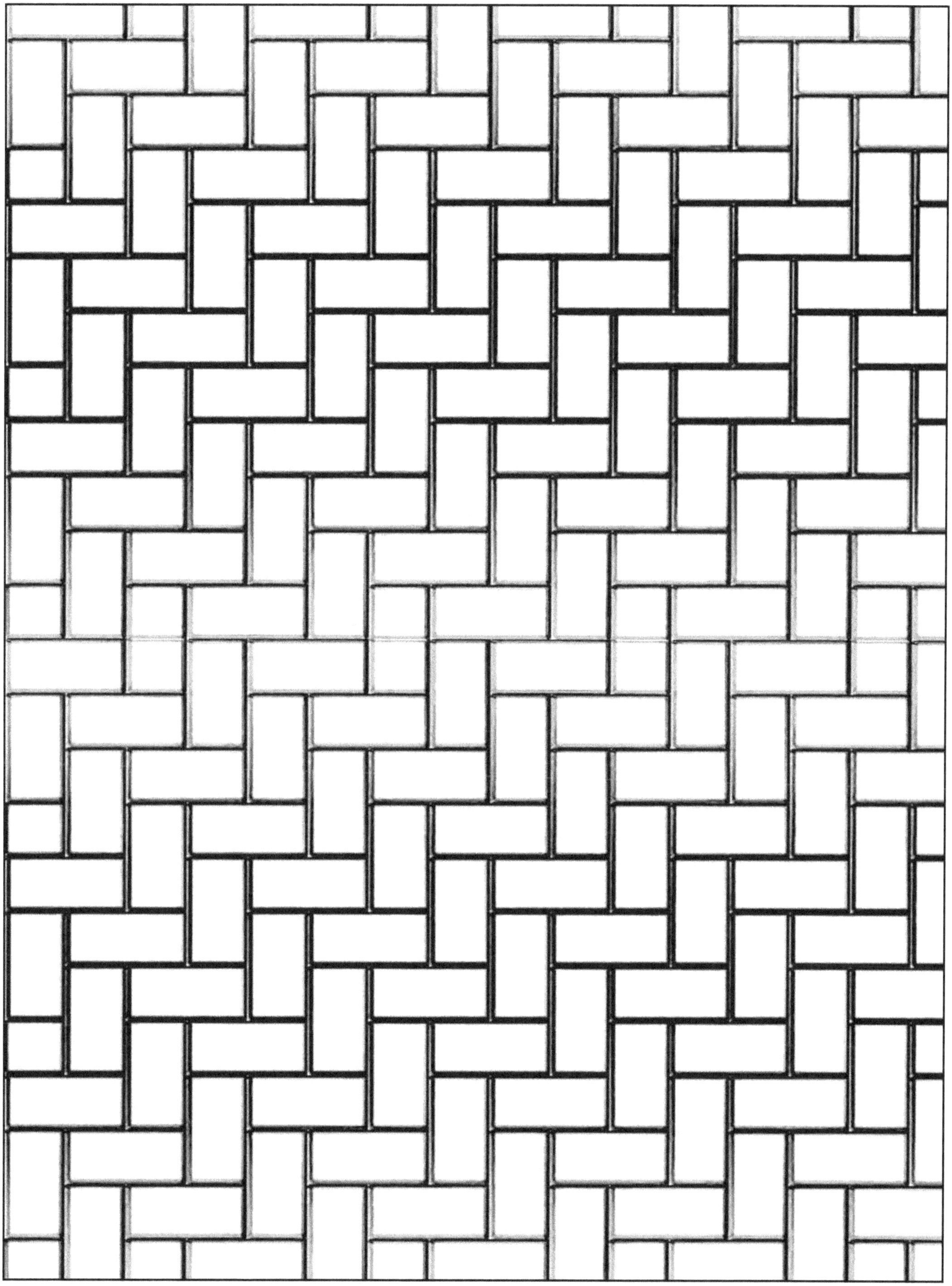

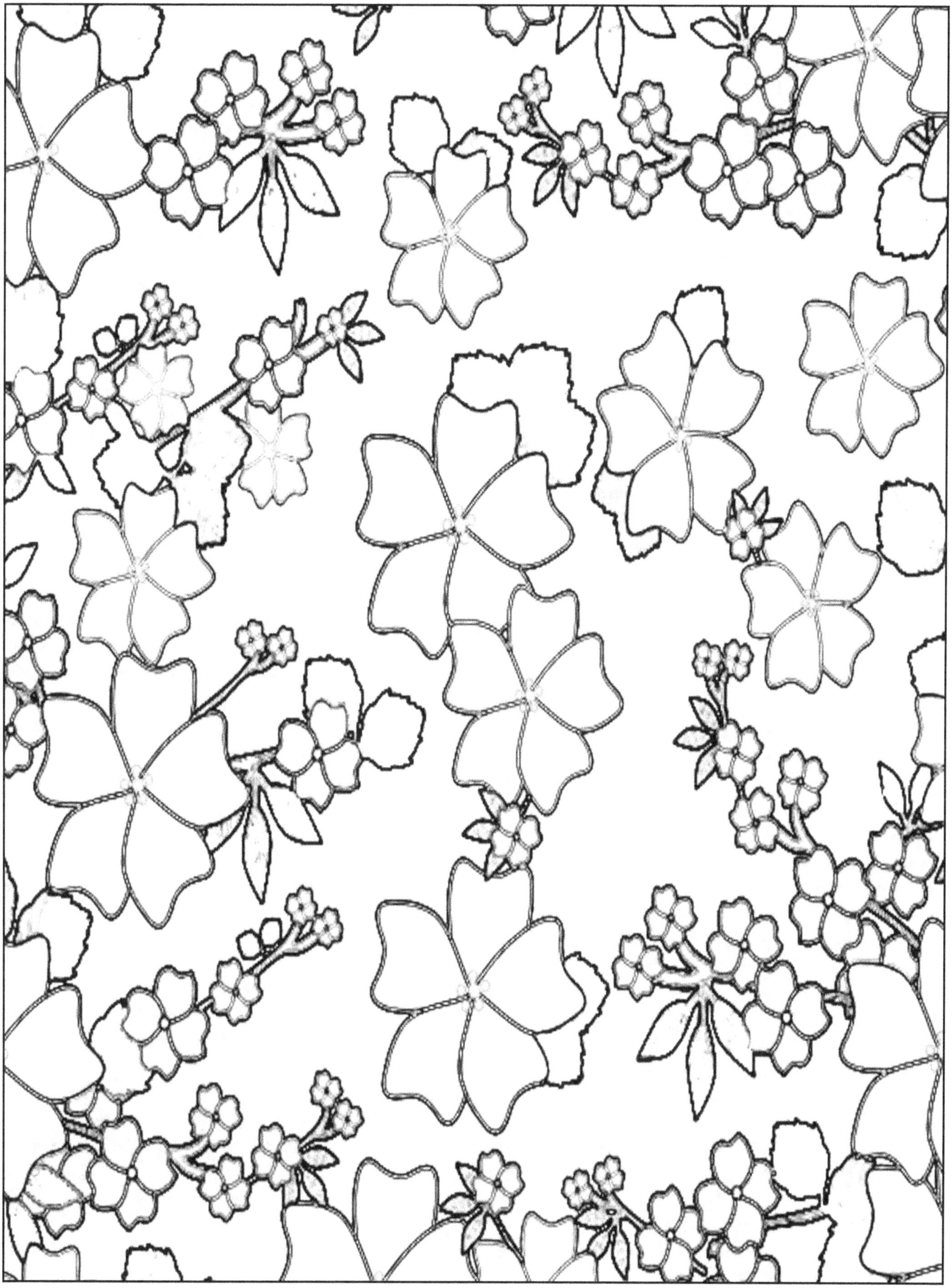

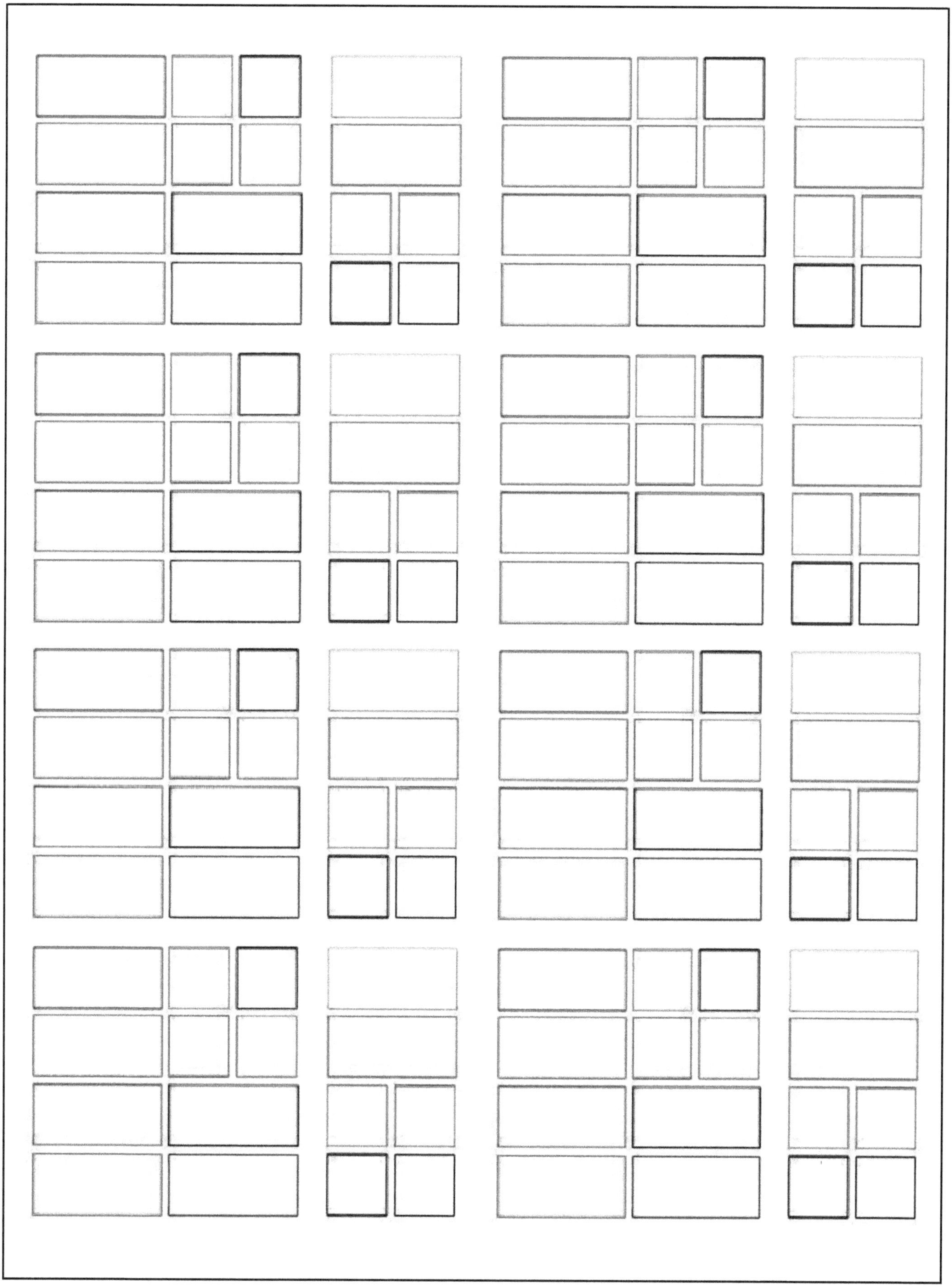

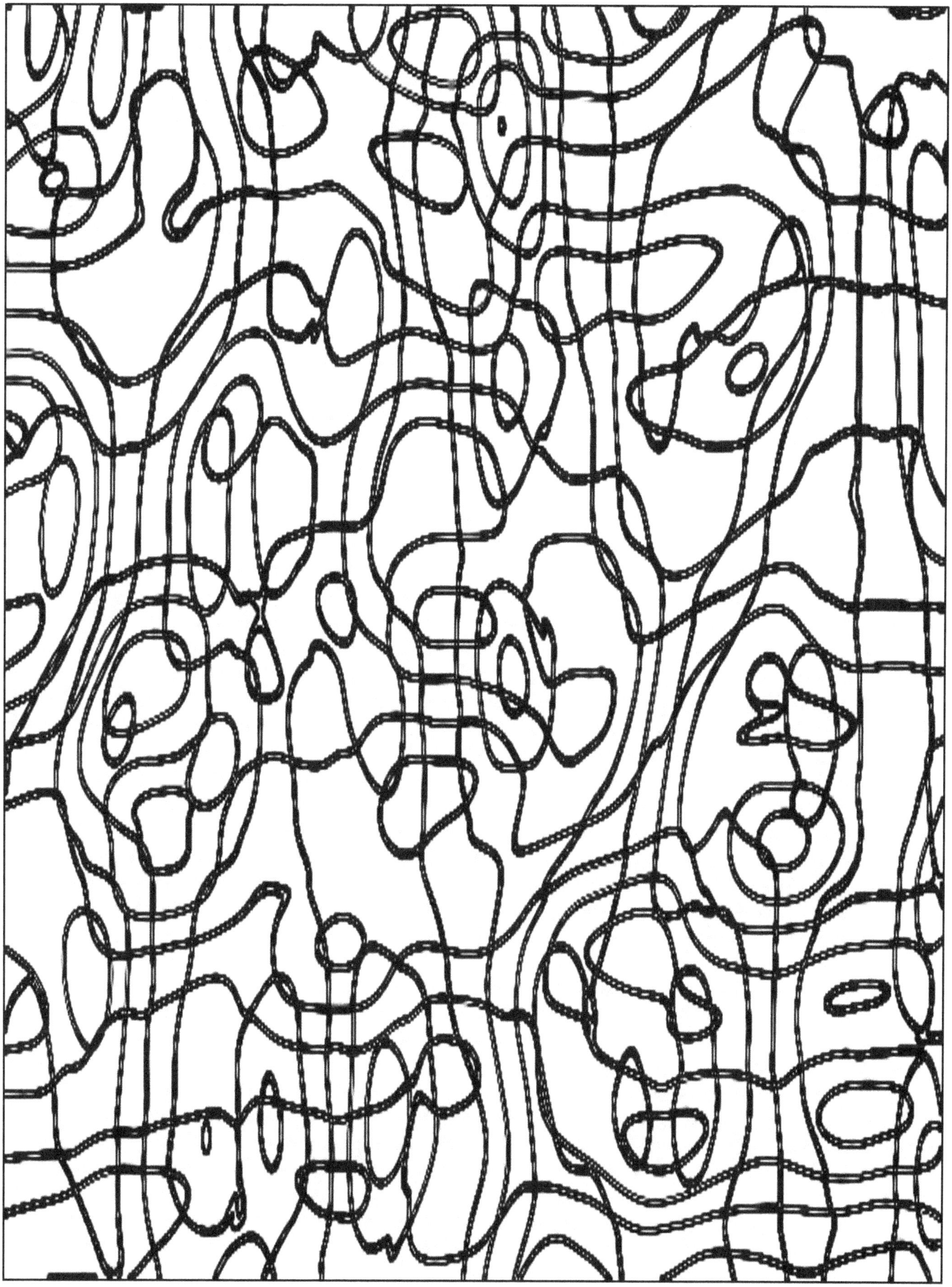

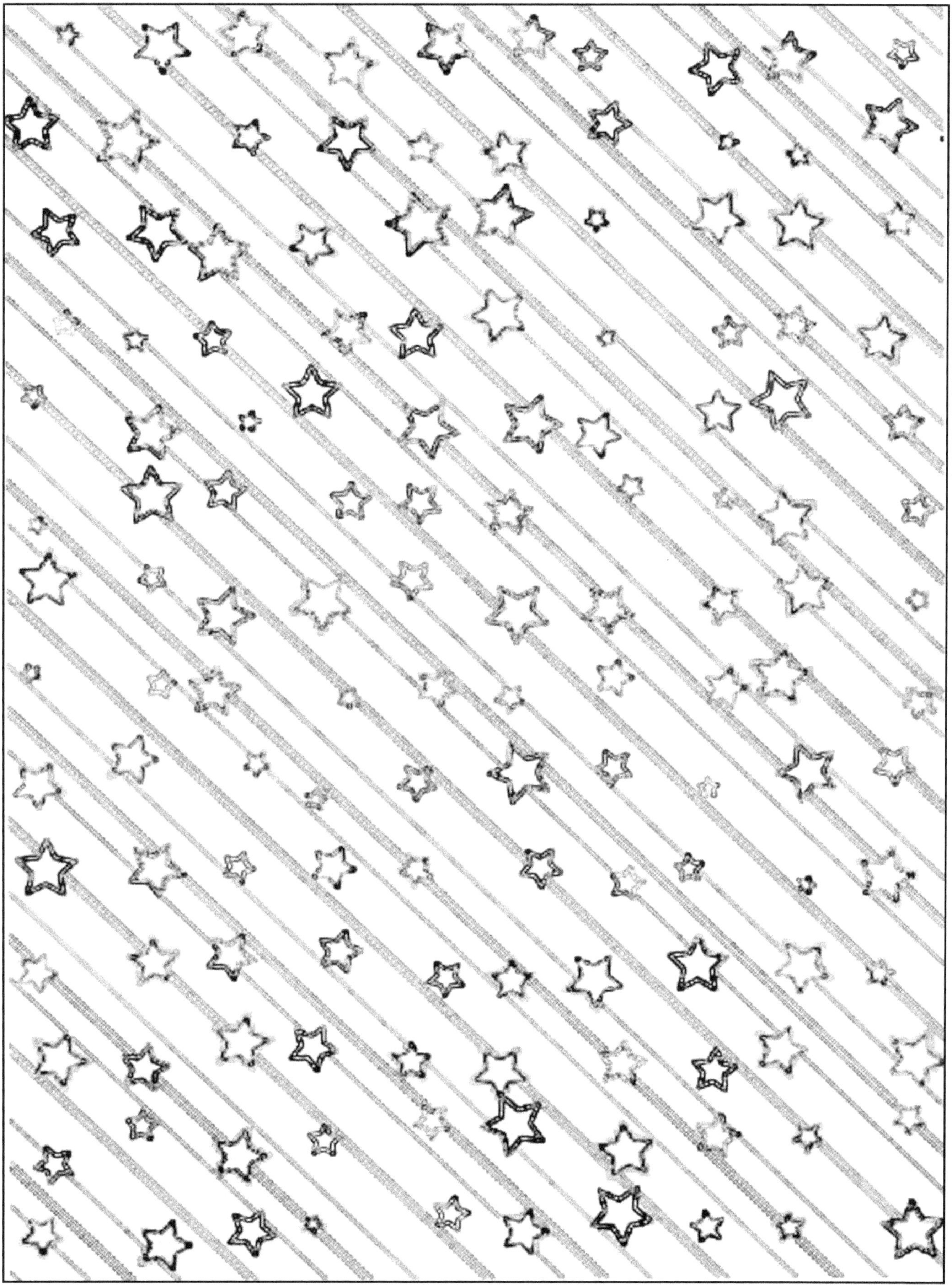

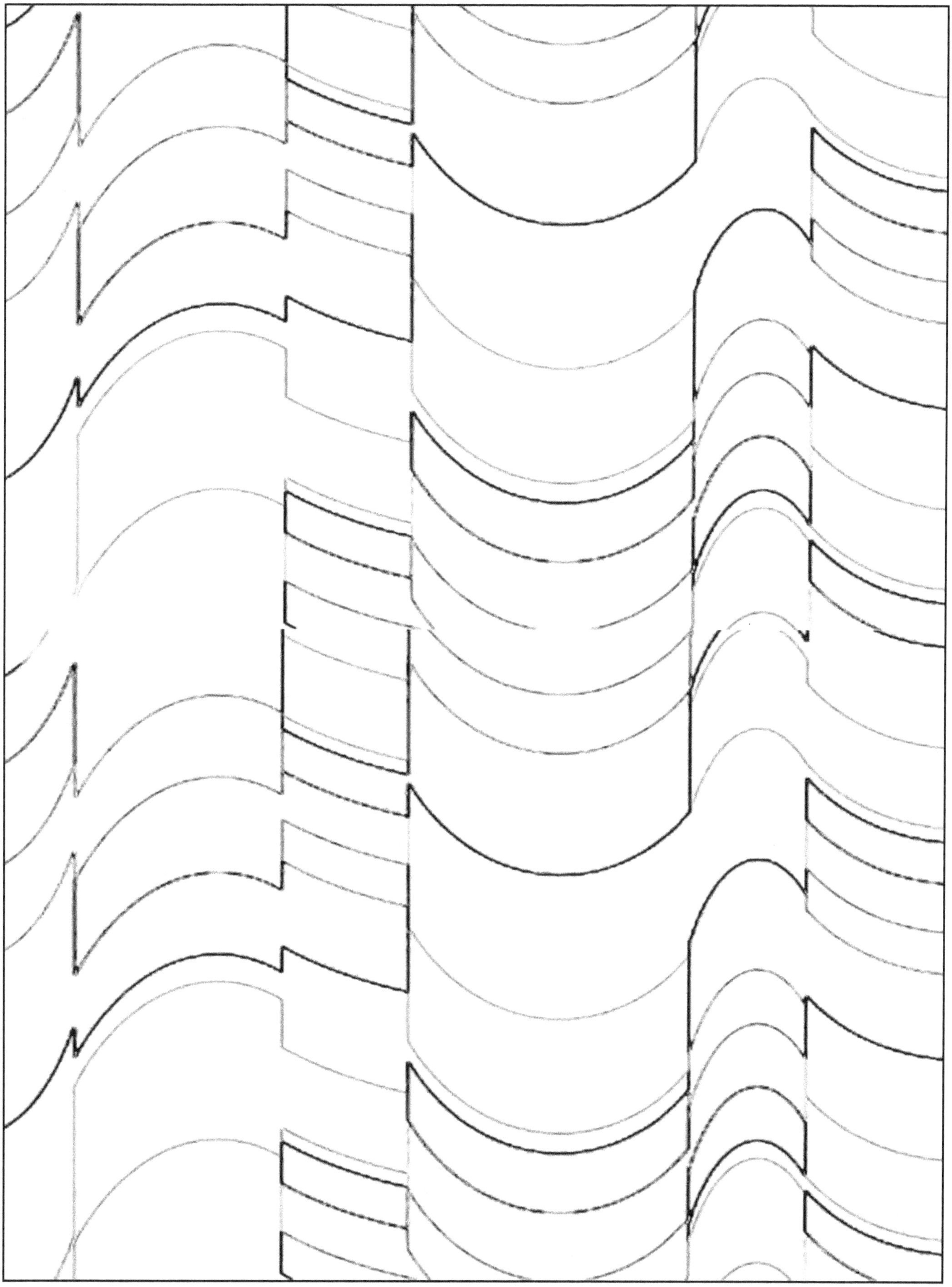

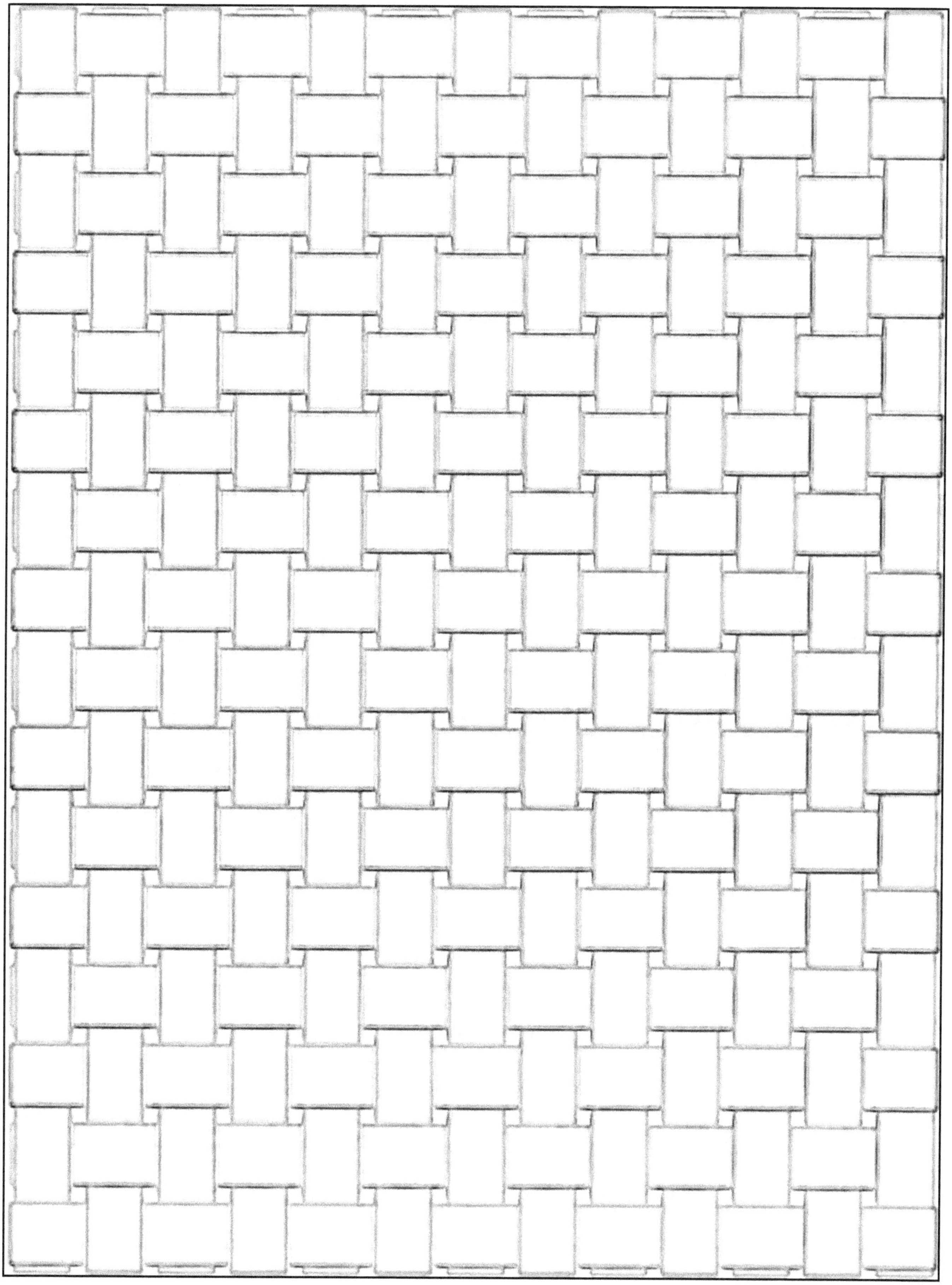

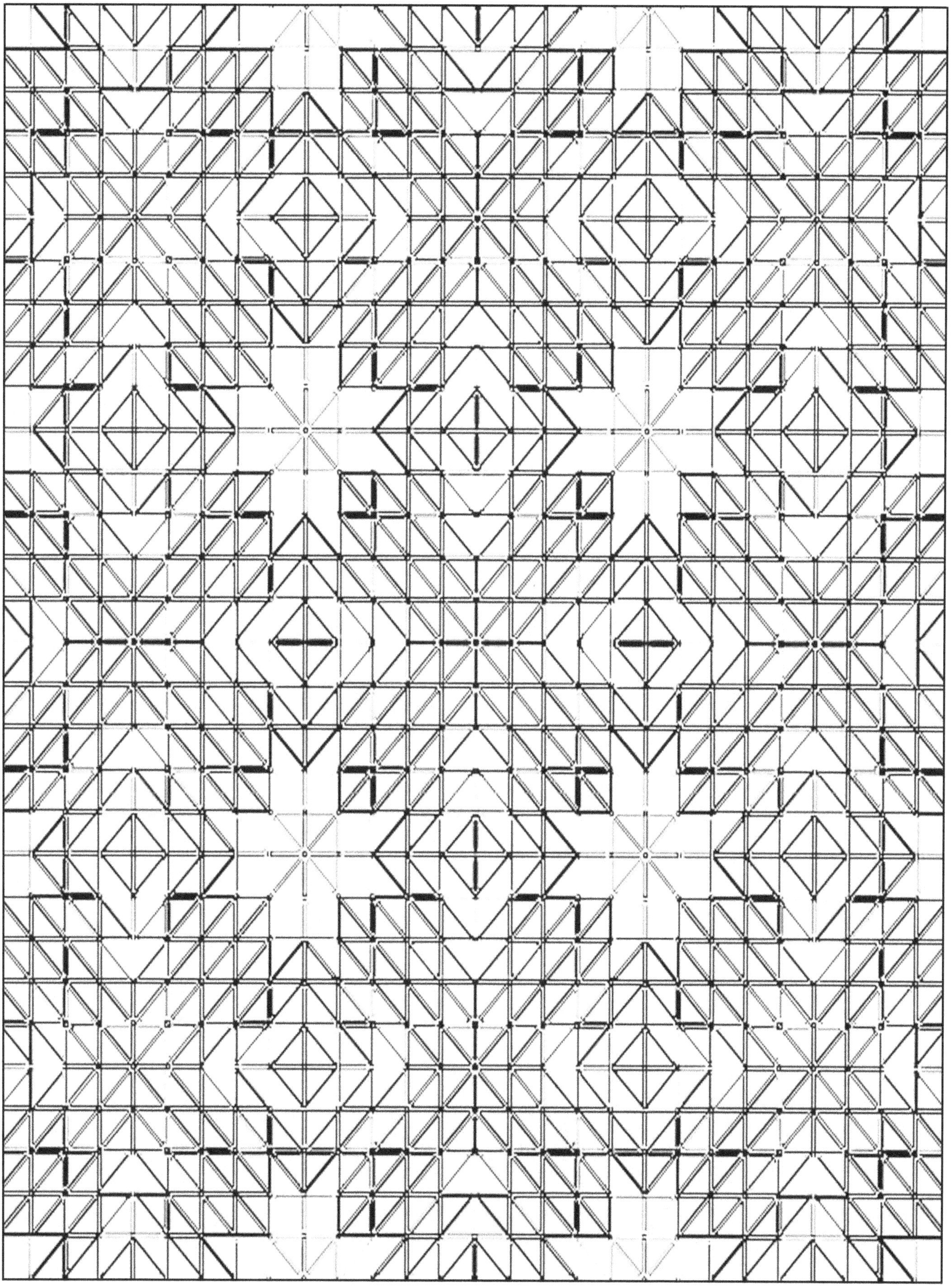

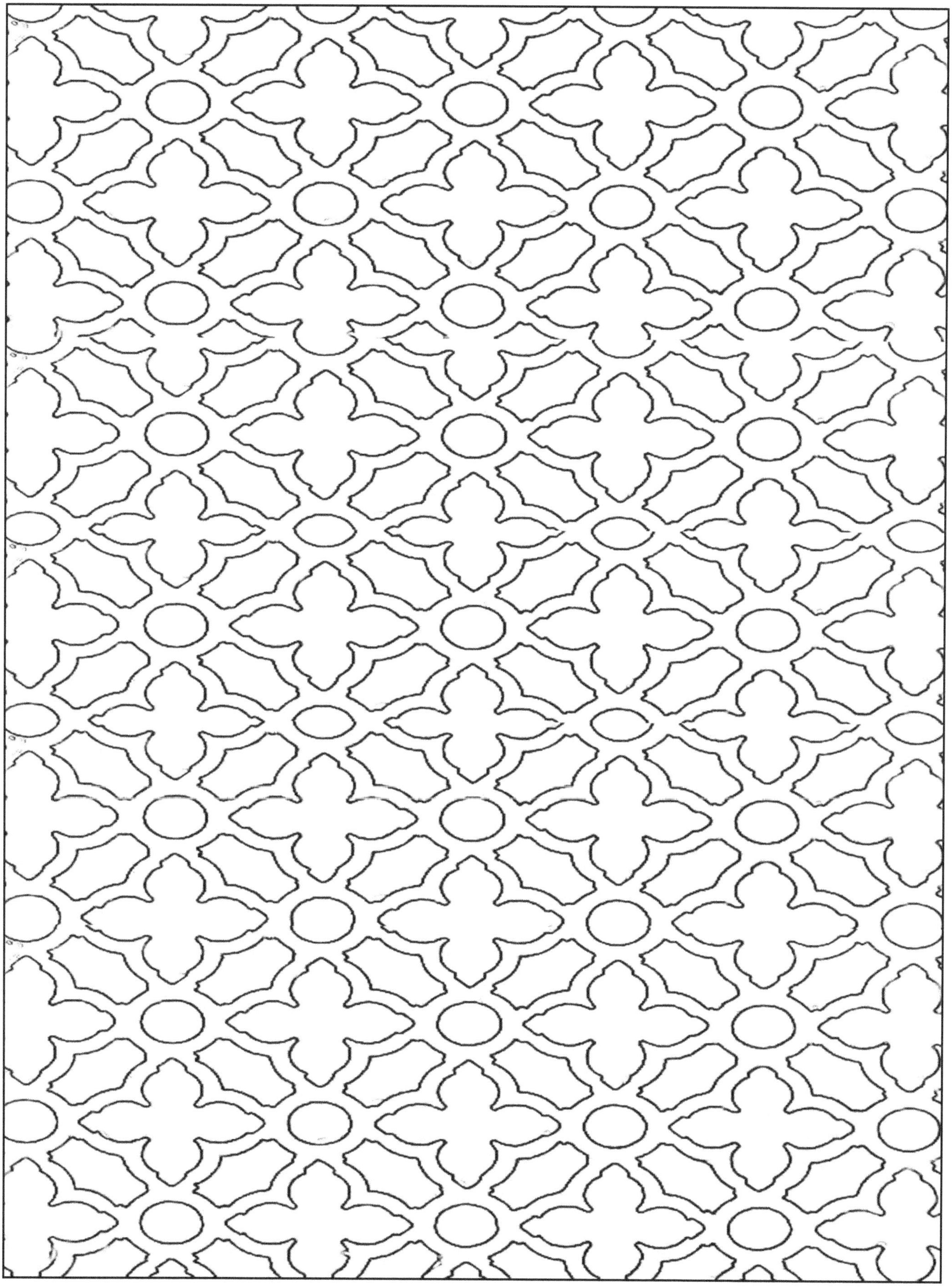

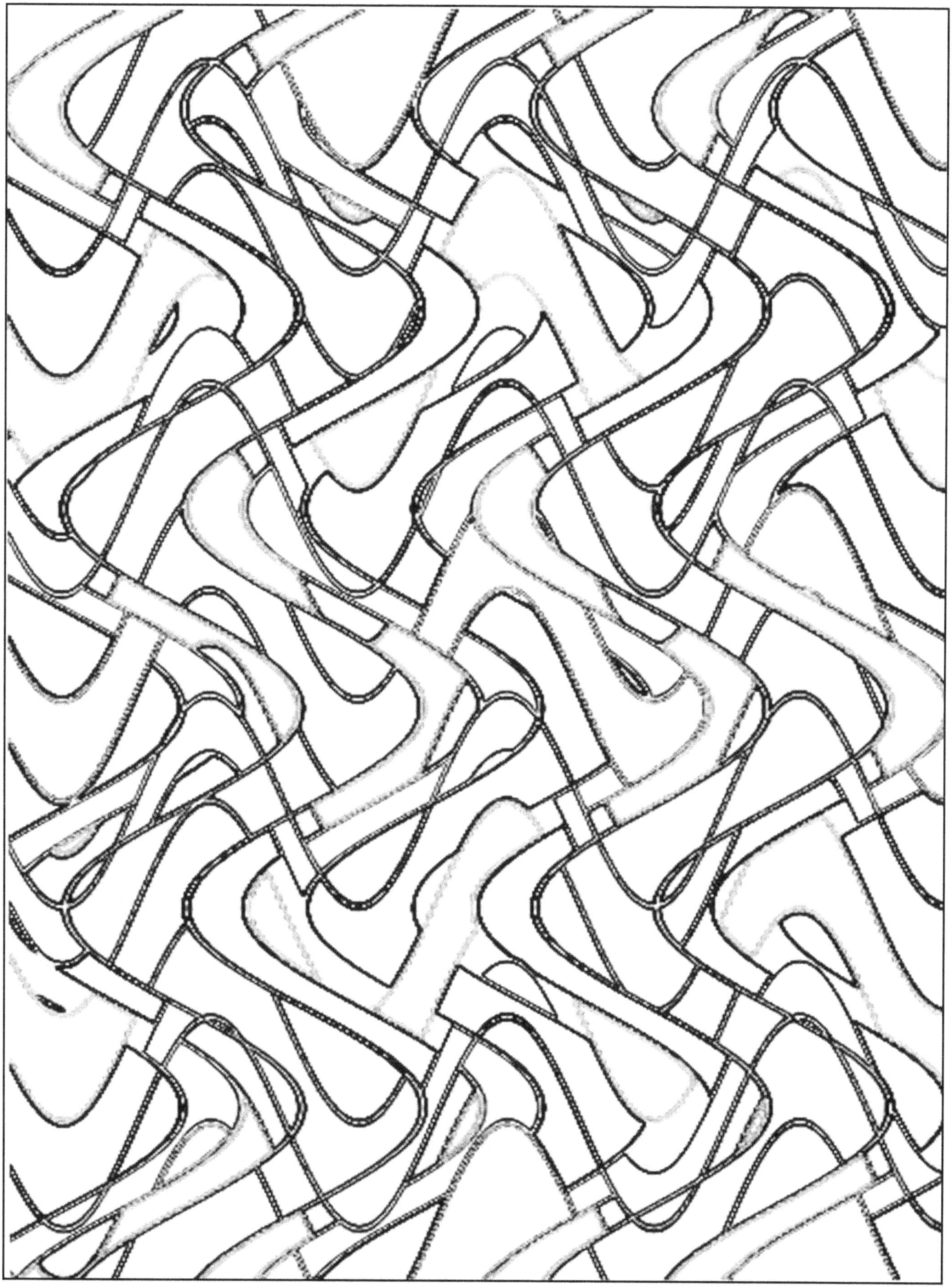

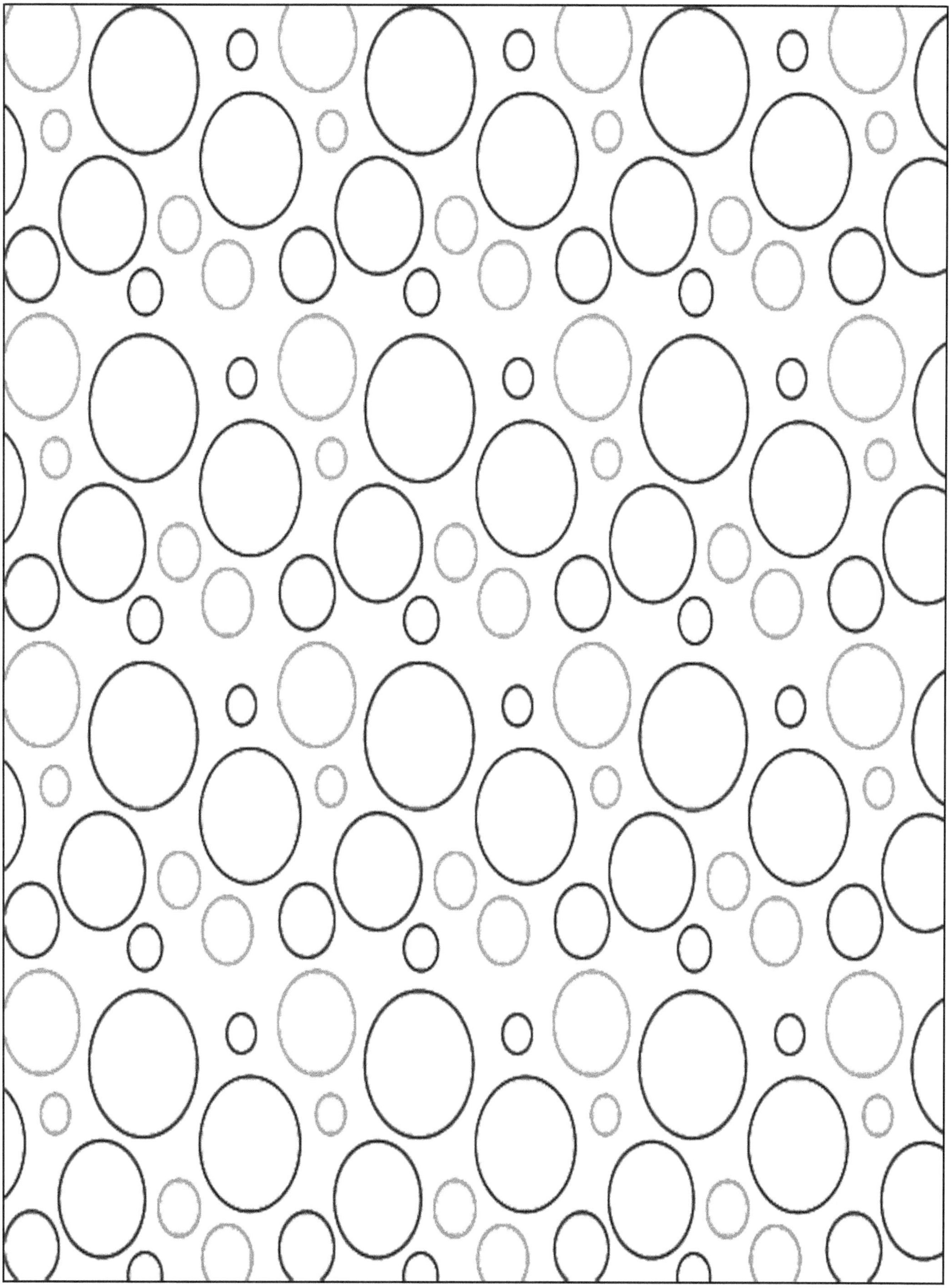

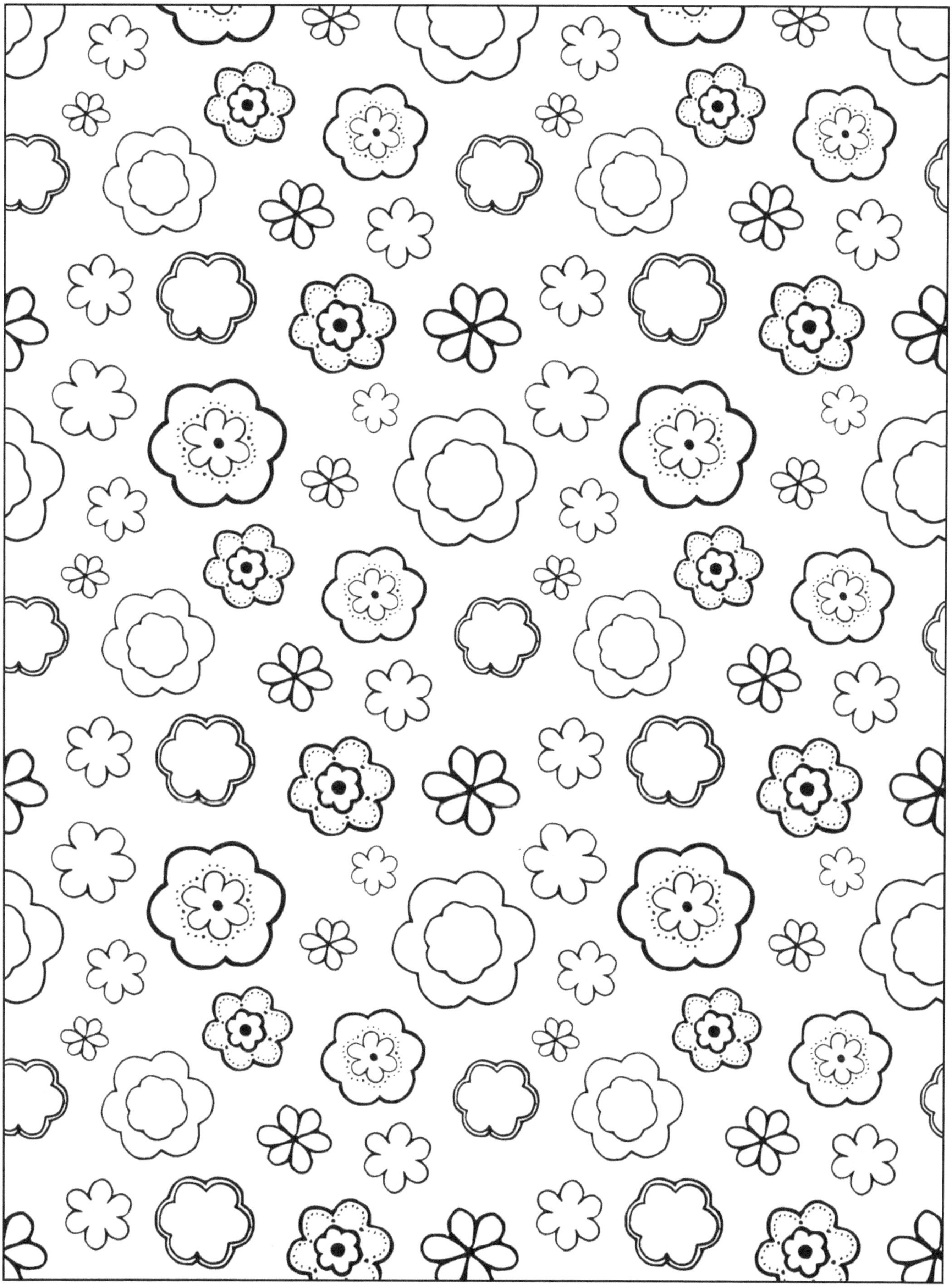

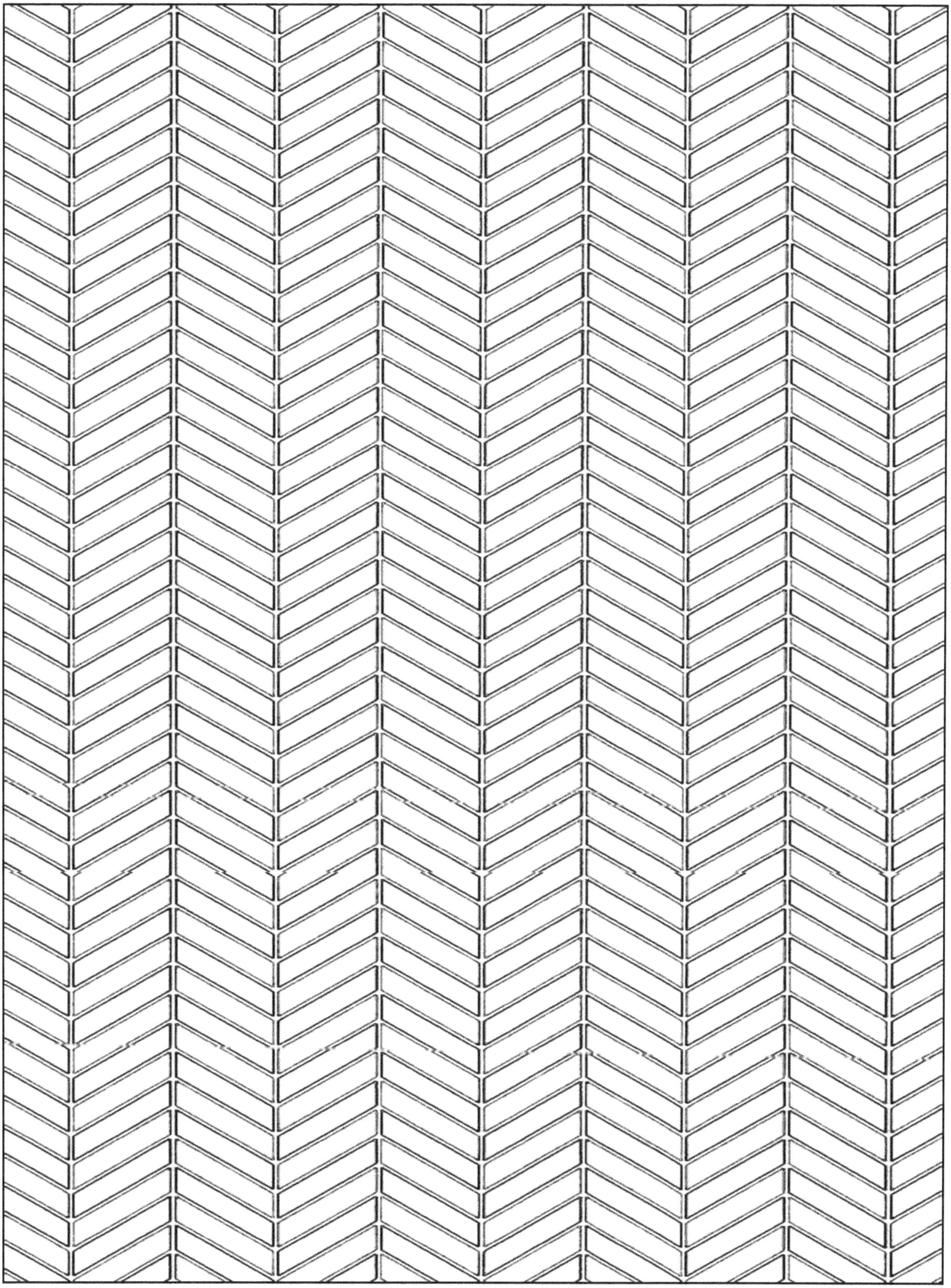

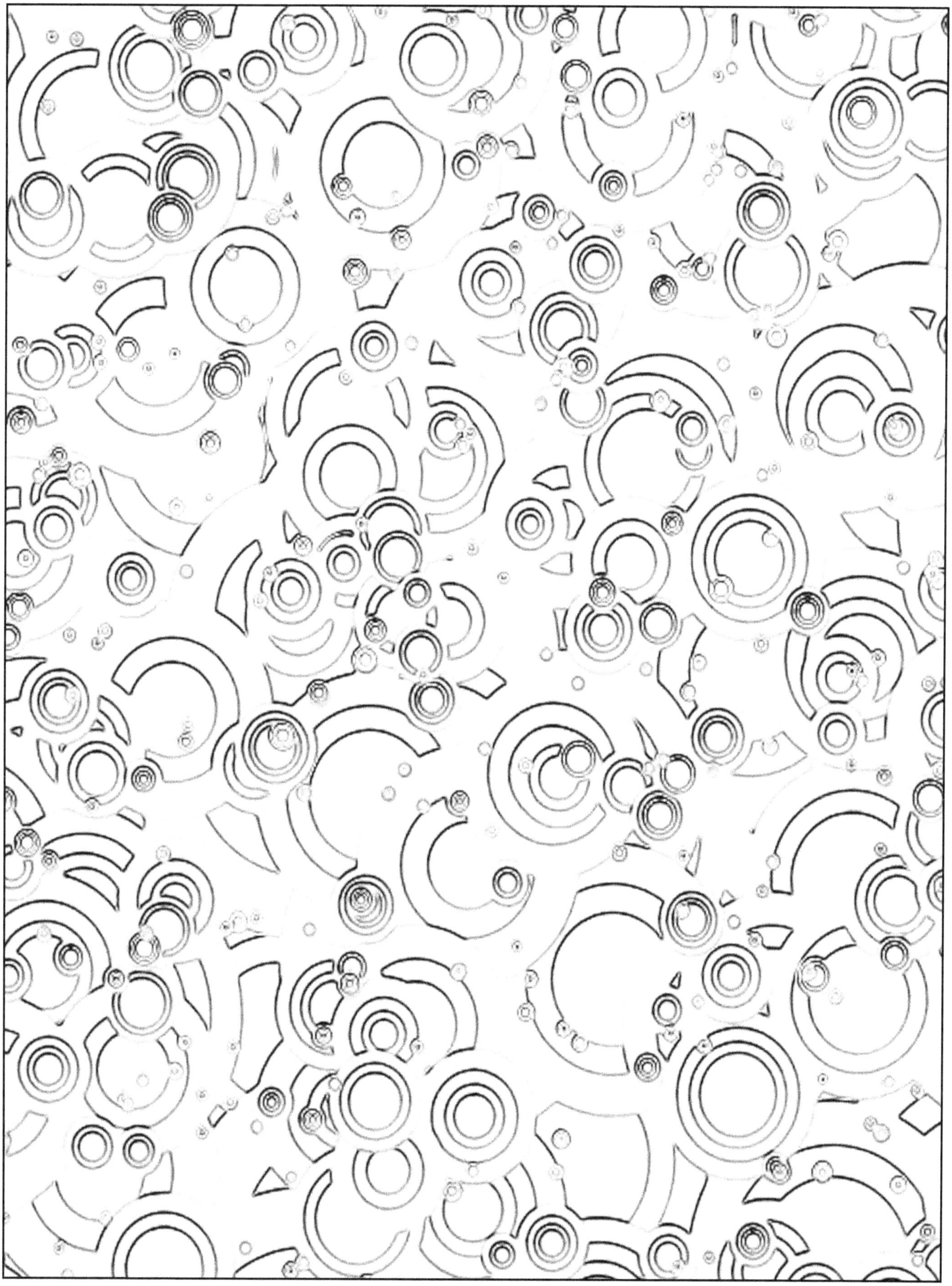

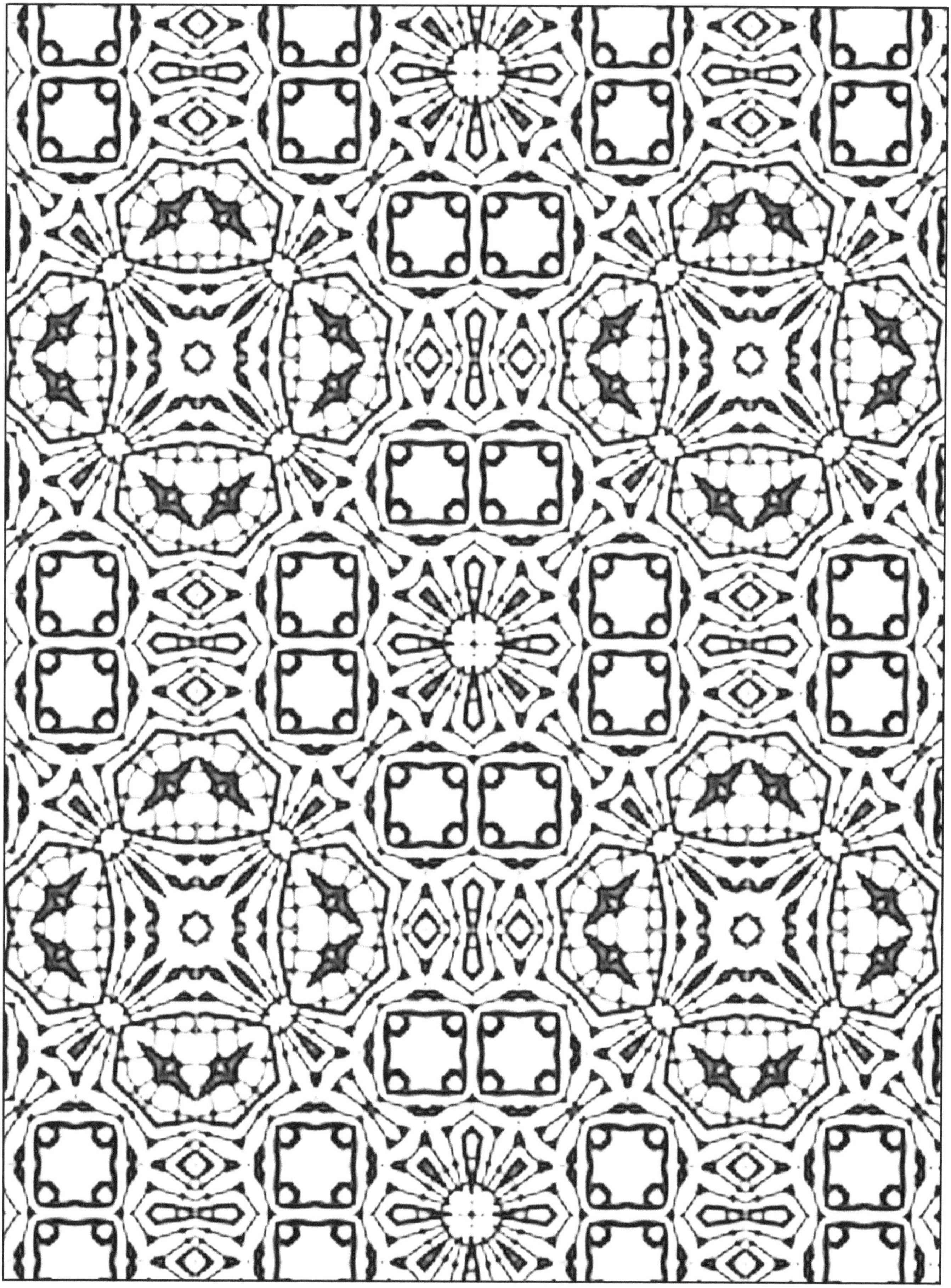

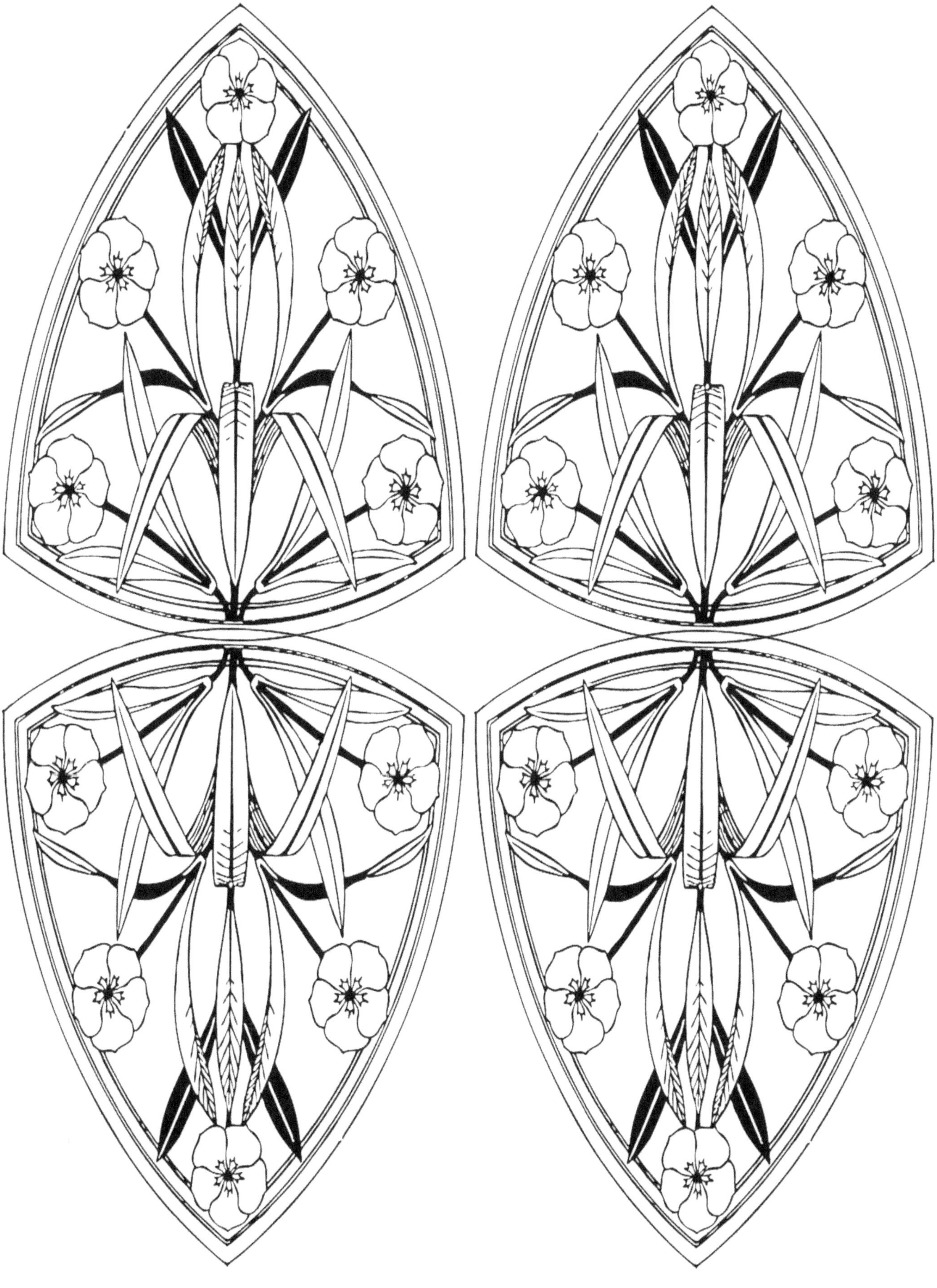

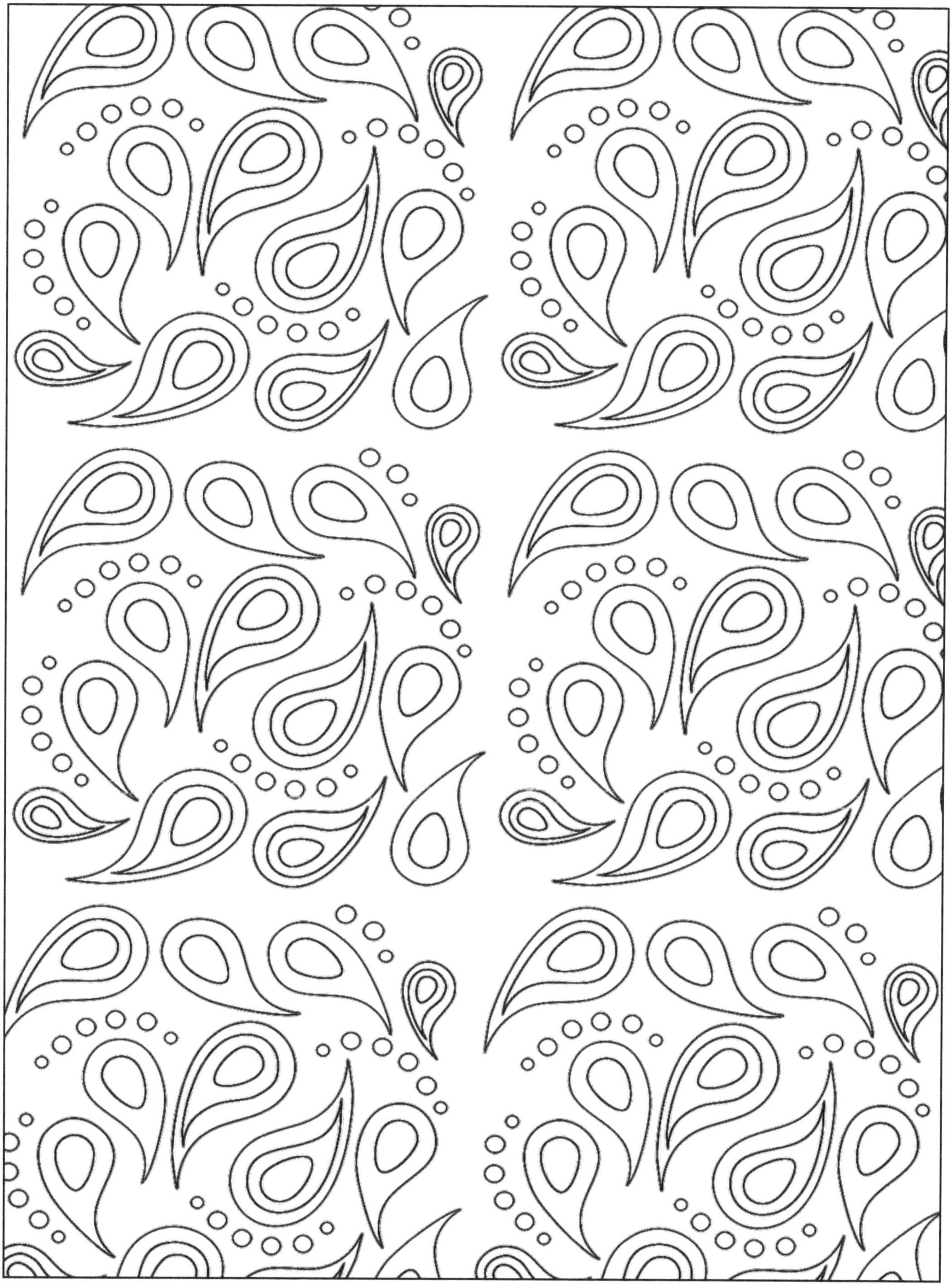

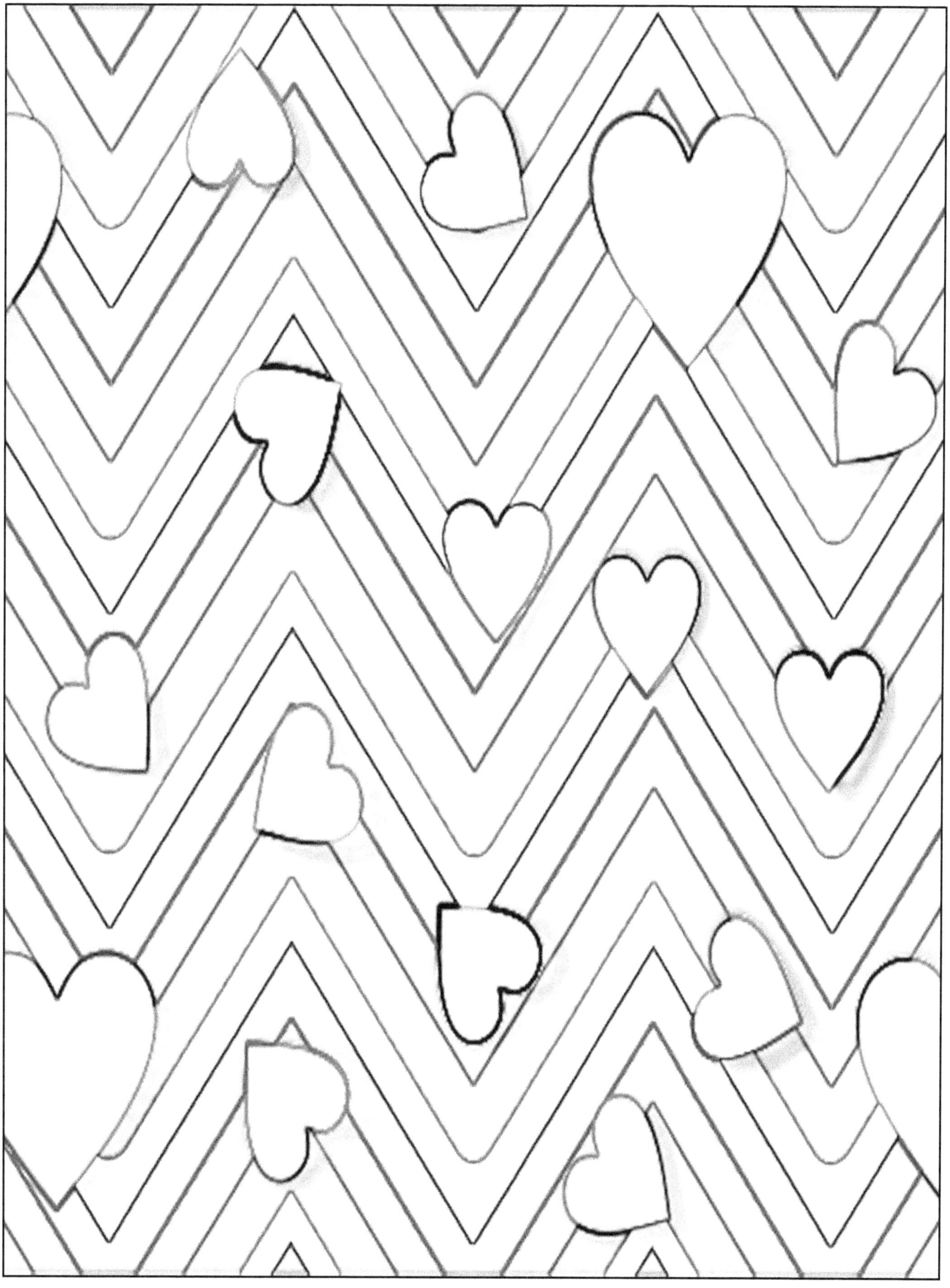

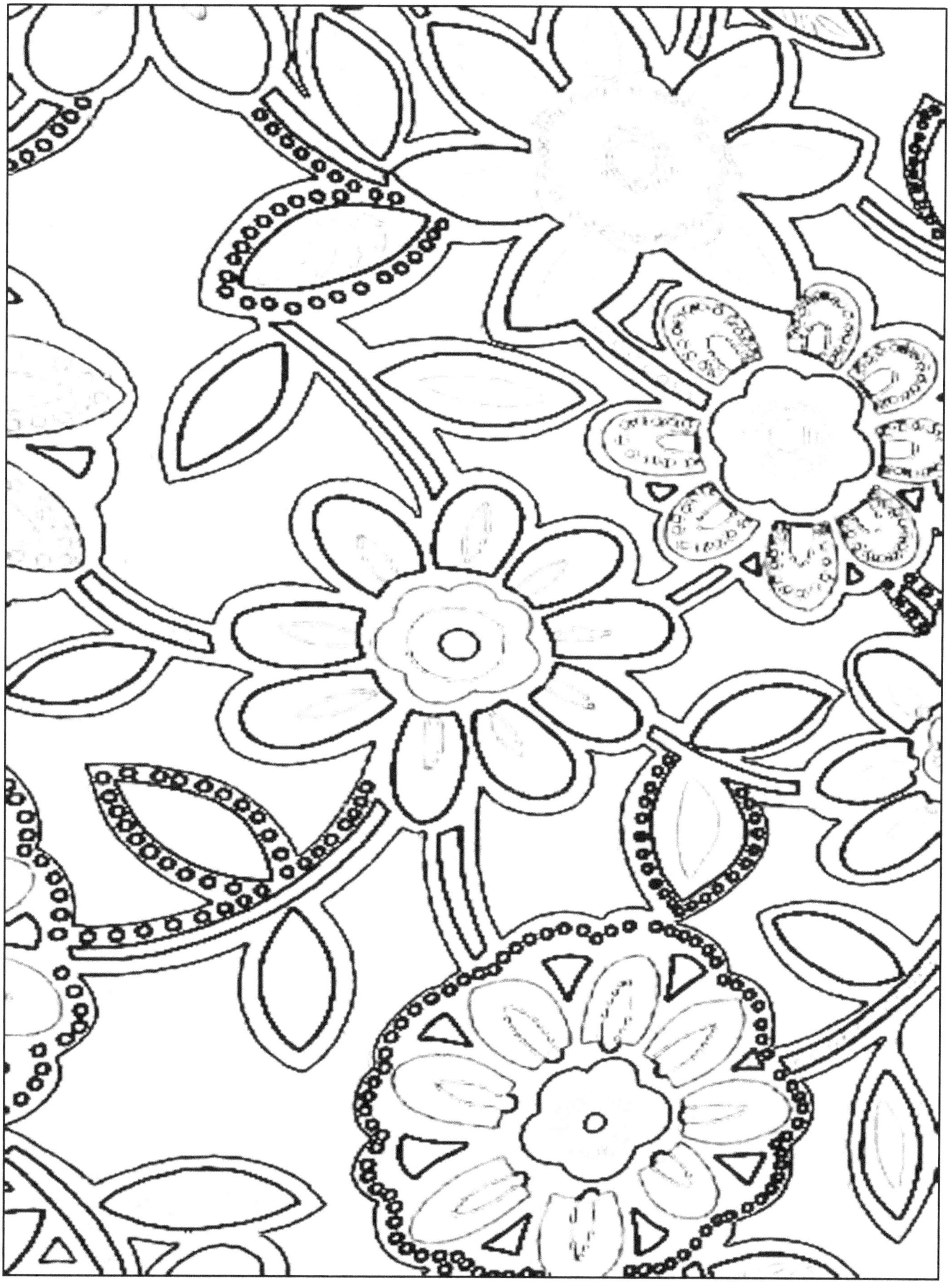

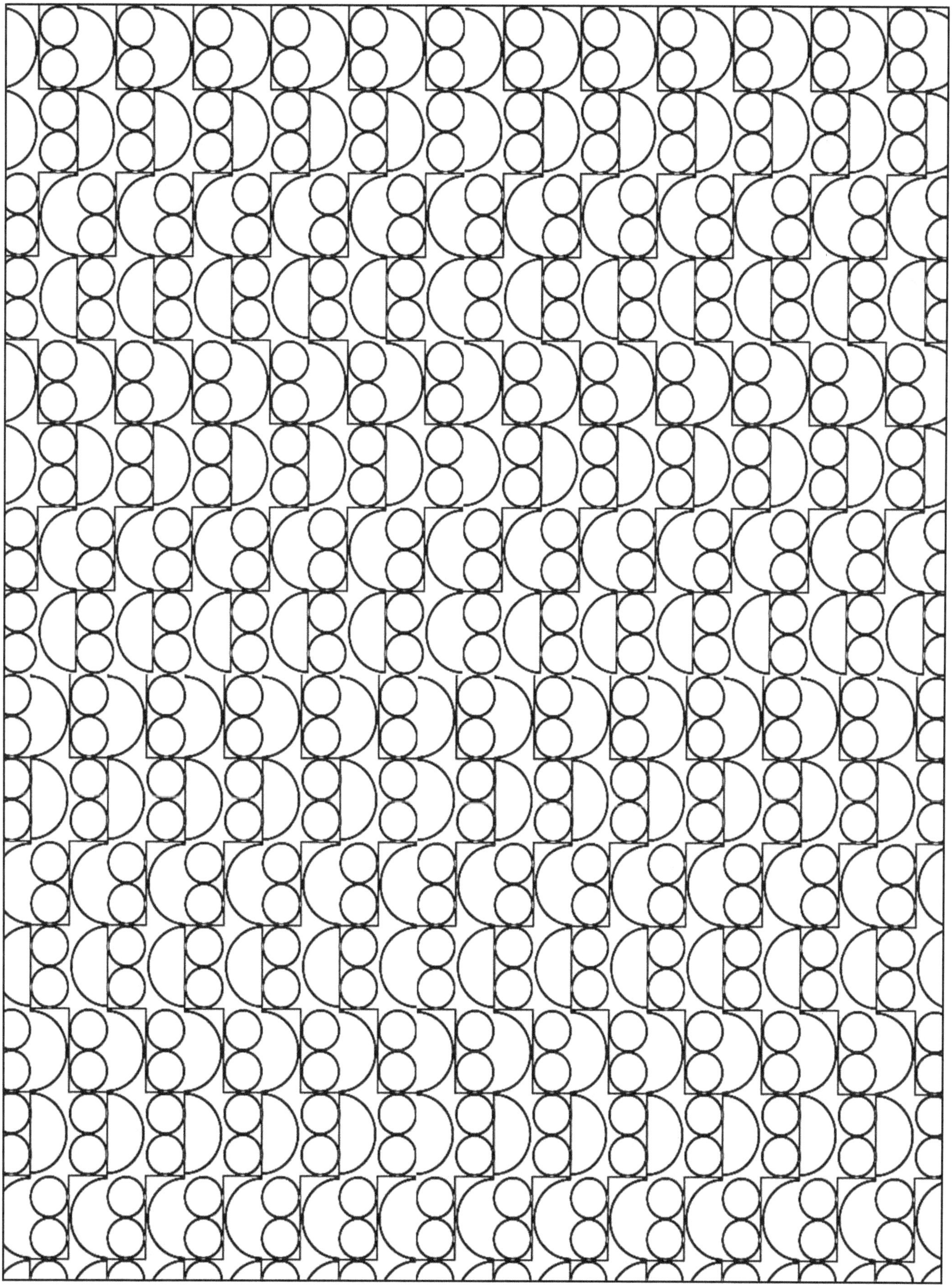

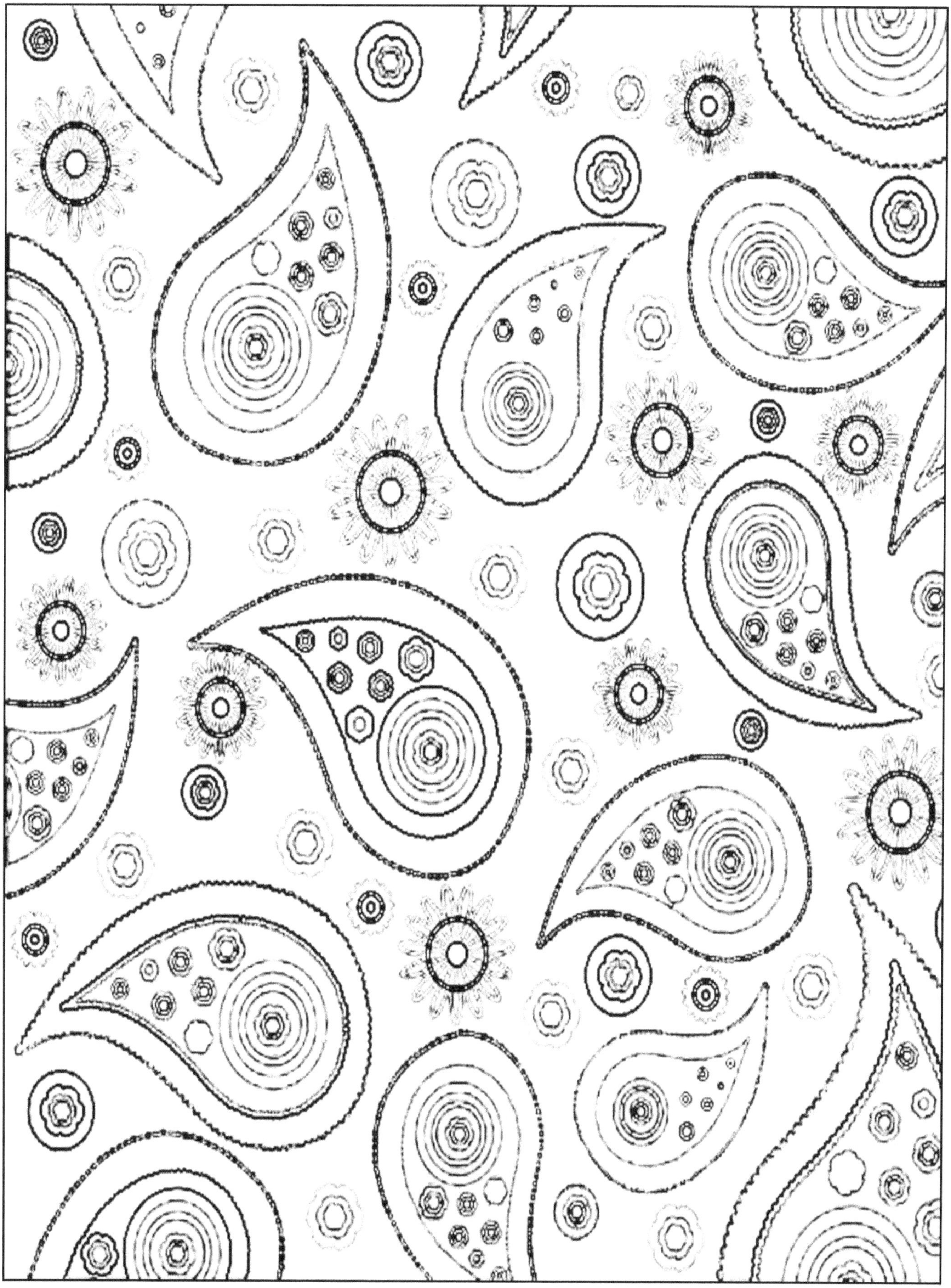

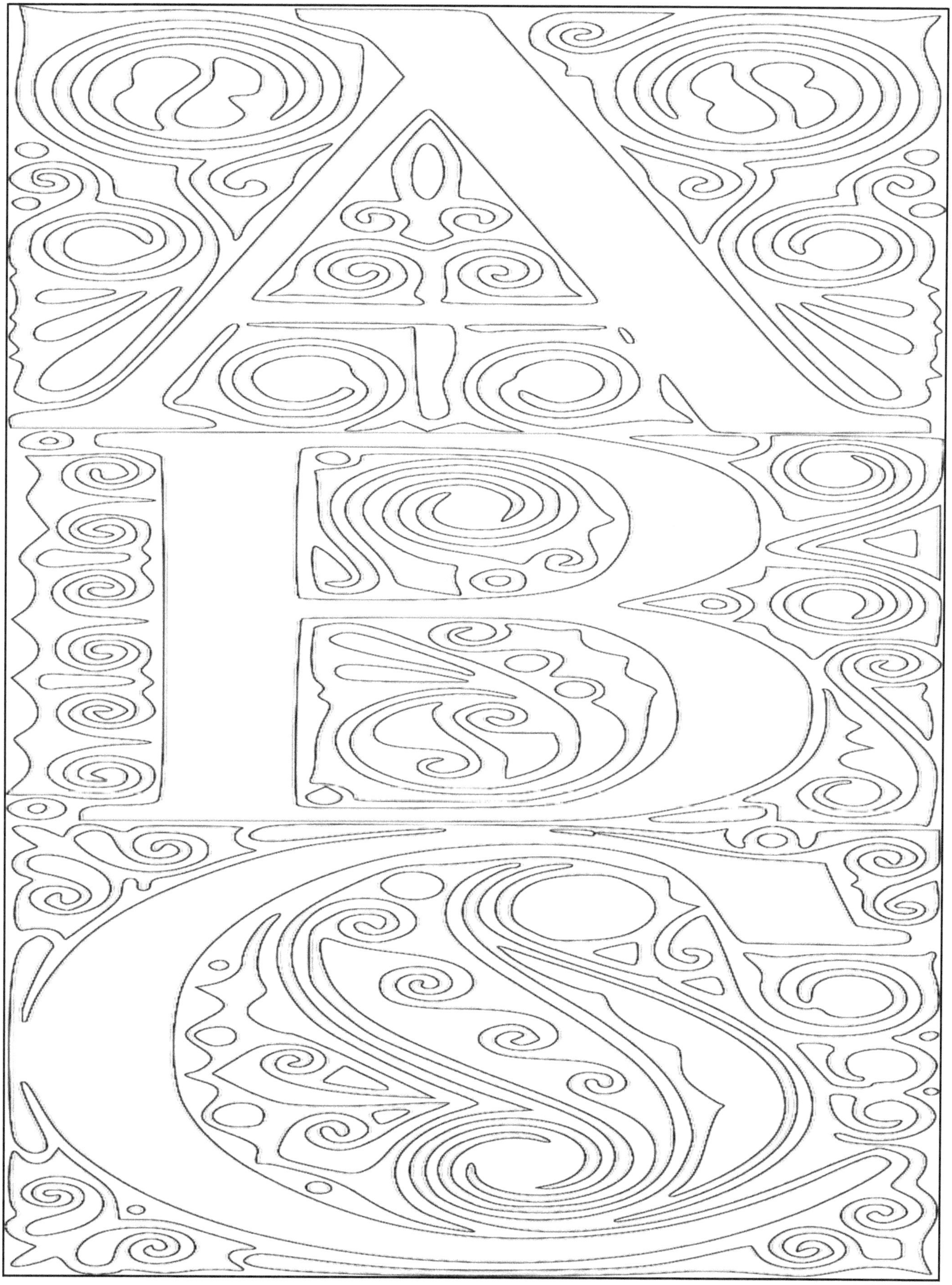
ABC

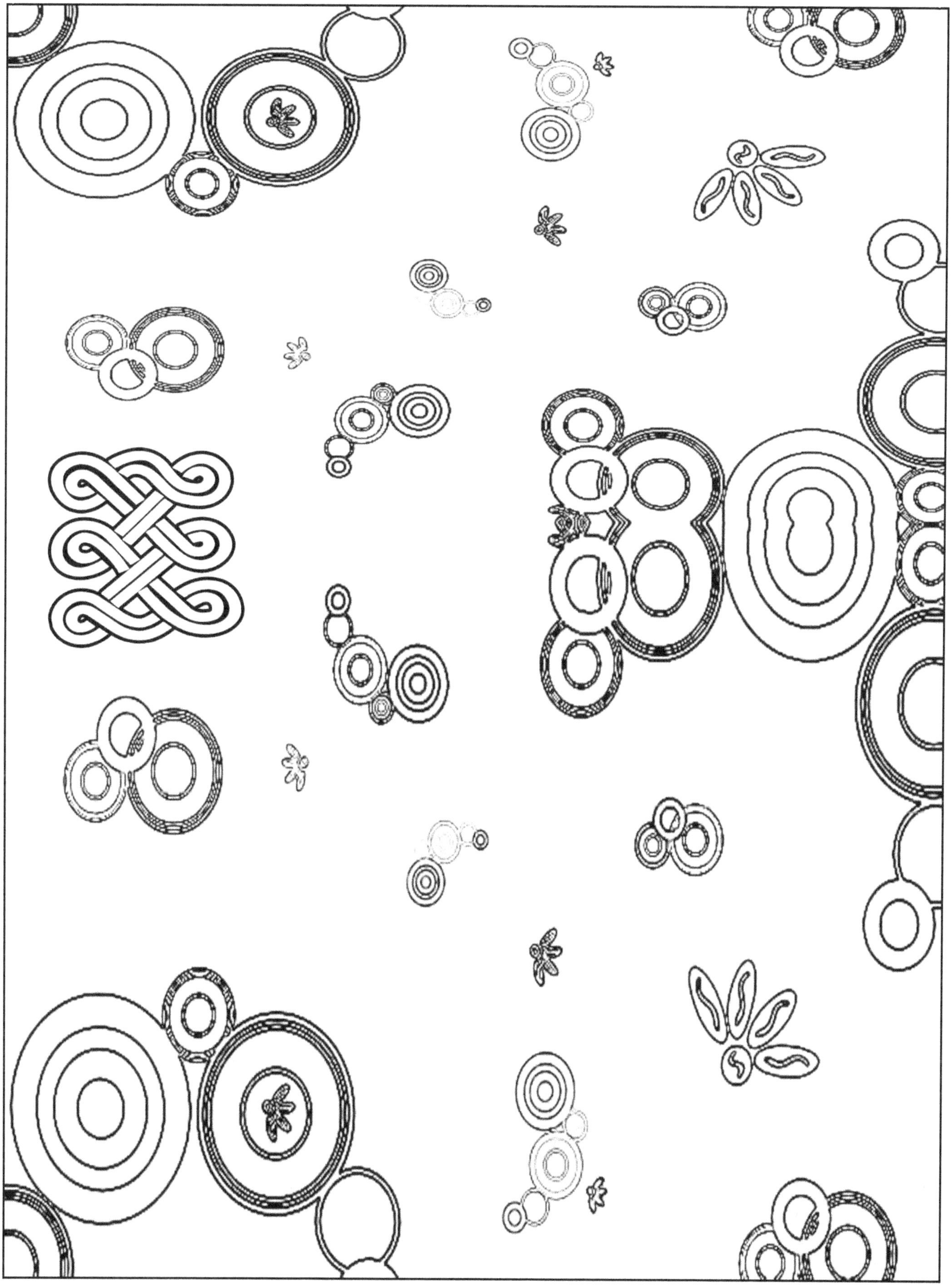

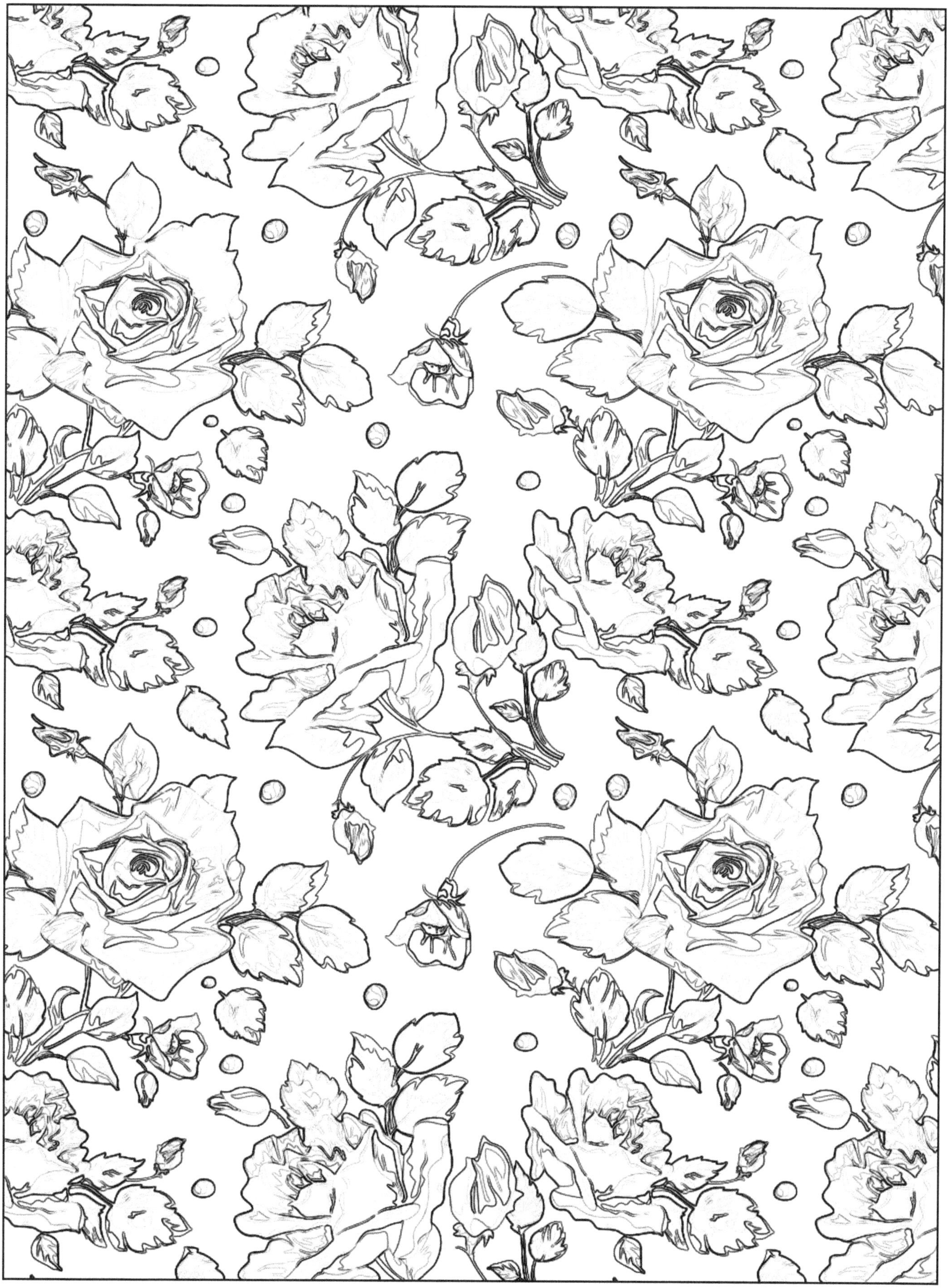

www.ingramcontent.com/pod-product-compliance
Lightning Source LLC
Chambersburg PA
CBHW080835180526
45168CB00006B/2694
* 9 7 8 1 5 1 2 1 2 9 8 9 2 *